Backbone of the Nation: Illustrated Biographies of 150 Influential People in Chinese History

Illustrations by Wang Xiaoshu
Poems by Zhang Shandong
English translations by Chen Yinan

汪晓曙 绘图
张山东 诗文
陈一楠 译

中国古代150位历史名人画传

华南理工大学出版社
·广州·

图书在版编目（CIP）数据

炎黄风骨：中国古代 150 位历史名人画传 / 汪晓曙绘图；张山东诗文；陈一楠译 .—广州：华南理工大学出版社，2018.8

ISBN 978-7-5623-5734-6

Ⅰ．①炎… Ⅱ．①汪… ②张… ③陈… Ⅲ．①历史人物—列传—中国—古代—画册 Ⅳ．① K820.2-64

中国版本图书馆 CIP 数据核字（2018）第 172851 号

炎黄风骨·中国古代 150 位历史名人画传

汪晓曙　绘图，张山东　诗文，陈一楠　译

出 版 人：	卢家明
出版发行：	华南理工大学出版社
	（广州五山华南理工大学 17 号楼，邮编：510640）
	http://www.scutpress.com.cn　　E-mail: scutc13@scut.edu.cn
	营销部电话：020-87113487　87111048（传真）
总 策 划：	毛润政
执行策划：	吴俊卿　蔡亚兰
责任编辑：	毛润政　王　倩
技术编辑：	吉超群
印 刷 者：	广州市新怡印务有限公司
开　　本：	787mm×1092m 1/12　印张：26　字数：410 千
版　　次：	2018 年 8 月第 1 版　2018 年 8 月第 1 次印刷
定　　价：	298.00 元

版权所有　盗版必究　　印装差错　负责调换

序 言 Preface

在亘古辽宽的神州大地上，渊源五千载，涌现出一大批仁人志士和英雄豪杰。他们为中华民族的生存与崛起、富强与兴旺，前赴后继，呕心沥血，砥砺前行，继往开来，成为炎黄子孙中杰出的精英和翘楚。他们或昂首于苍穹之上，或鼎足于大地之间，或屹立于世界之巅，或雄踞于民族之林，在汹涌澎湃的人类历史长河中搏击惊涛骇浪，在浩瀚无垠的历史星空中闪烁出夺目的光芒，建构起中华民族永恒的精神家园，成为中华民族的灵魂和脊梁，让炎黄血脉偾张，让华夏蒉庭高筑，扬名四海。

《炎黄风骨·中国古代150位历史名人画传》通过画、诗、文及英文翻译四种文学艺术形式，图文并茂地把中国五千年文明史展现给广大读者。纵观浩如烟海的中华文明发展进程，站在历史的高度，从那些充满聪明才智、充满英雄气概和民族气节，并为中华崛起做出巨大贡献的众多历史人物中，遴选出150位具有代表性、典型性的中国古代英豪贤达，绘制成精美的图画，配上咏颂的诗歌，并撰写简练的人物介绍（含中、英文），同时精选出与历史人物相关的精彩诗文或名言，编辑成一部集艺术性、文学性、学术性、教育性、可读性为一体的画传体图书，为创造了五千年文明史的旷世英杰树碑立传，以颂华夏精神，以咏炎黄风骨。

In China's 5000 years of history, many heroes have risen to the challenge and sustained the nation when it was at stake. They strove tirelessly toward China's rejuvenation, brought China glories, and led it to where it stands today. It was them who made the Chinese nation a proud and active member of the world. The tales of these heroes were handed down from generation to generation and resound throughout the land even today. They were the reason behind China's splendid history and we revere them as the backbone of the Chinese nation.

In Backbone of the Nation: Illustrated Biographies of 150 Influential People in Chinese History, we seek to portray the colorful history of China in diverse forms by incorporating illustrations, poems, and biographies in Chinese and English. We have, out of the numerous prominent historical figures who have made significant contributions to the rise of the Chinese nation, selected 150 influential figures who we think best embody China's national spirits and have had tribute poems composed for them. This book also contains exquisite illustrations and brief bilingual biographies of the figures. We hope that

本书由著名画家汪晓曙教授精心绘制丹青，著名历史学者、诗人张山东先生撰文赋诗，陈一楠老师负责人物介绍部分的翻译，由华南理工大学出版社出版。他们创造性地展现了中华民族优秀传统文化的思想精华和道德精髓，不仅有利于弘扬中国优秀传统文化、讴歌华夏文明、颂扬炎黄风骨、传承民族精神，而且有利于广大读者更好地理解和把握以爱国主义为核心的民族精神和以改革创新为核心的时代精神。相信这些传播正能量、颂扬华夏英杰的150幅人物画传，能够为广大受众所喜爱和推崇。这正是响应习近平总书记提出的"勠力同心为实现'两个一百年'奋斗目标，实现中华民族伟大复兴的中国梦而努力奋斗"的号召，用艺以载道、文以化人的方式对"再承传统、不忘初心、复兴中华、砥砺前行"精神的积极响应与践行。以此致敬中华历代先贤英烈，弘扬祖国传统文化，从而坚定我们的文化自信，走进新时代，共圆中国梦。

许钦松

中国美协副主席、广东省文联主席
2018年7月

readers find this book educative, readable, and of artistic value.

The poems in this book were composed by Mr. Zhang Shandong and the illustrations were created by Professor Wang Xiaoshu. The biographies were translated into English by Mr. Chen Yinan. The book is published by South China University of Technology Press. The creators and editors of this book have made a huge effort to promote China' traditional culture and national ethos. We hope this book could serve as a response to President Xi Jinping's call for all Chinese to strive with one heart to achieve the "two centenary goals" and realize the Chinese Dream of national rejuvenation.

Vice-president of China Artists Association,
President of Guangdong Federation of Literary and Art Circles
Xu Qinsong
July 2018

目录 Contents

002	三皇五帝	The Three Sovereigns and Five Emperors
004	女娲	Nüwa
006	唐尧	Yao
008	虞舜	Shun
010	夏禹	Yu
012	皋陶	Gao Yao
014	仓颉	Cang Jie
016	杜康	Du Kang
018	伊尹	Yi Yin
020	姬昌	Ji Chang
022	姜尚	Jiang Shang
024	李耳	Li Er
026	伍员	Wu Yuan
028	鲁班	Lu Ban
030	孔子	Confucius
032	孙武	Sun Wu
034	范蠡	Fan Li
036	西施	Xi Shi
038	勾践	Goujian
040	墨翟	Mo Di
042	商鞅	Shang Yang
044	孟母	Meng Mu
046	孟子	Mencius
048	庄子	Zhuangzi
050	屈原	Qu Yuan
052	嬴政	Ying Zheng
054	李斯	Li Si
056	蒙恬	Meng Tian
058	刘邦	Liu Bang
060	项羽	Xiang Yu
062	张良	Zhang Liang
064	卓文君	Zhuo Wenjun
066	周亚夫	Zhou Yafu
068	张骞	Zhang Qian
070	李广	Li Guang
072	刘彻	Liu Che
074	苏武	Su Wu
076	司马迁	Sima Qian
078	李陵	Li Ling
080	王昭君	Wang Zhaojun
082	张衡	Zhang Heng
084	张道陵	Zhang Daoling
086	蔡伦	Cai Lun
088	张仲景	Zhang Zhongjing
090	曹操	Cao Cao
092	貂蝉	Diao Chan
094	诸葛亮	Zhuge Liang
096	班固	Ban Gu
098	班超	Ban Chao
100	华佗	Hua Tuo
102	蔡琰	Cai Yan
104	张芝	Zhang Zhi
106	卫铄	Wei Shuo
108	王羲之	Wang Xizhi
110	谢安	Xie An
112	陶渊明	Tao Yuanming
114	许逊	Xu Xun
116	谢灵运	Xie Lingyun
118	祖冲之	Zu Chongzhi
120	郦道元	Li Daoyuan
122	贾思勰	Jia Sixie
124	李靖	Li Jing
126	魏徵	Wei Zheng
128	孙思邈	Sun Simiao
130	李世民	Li Shimin
132	玄奘	Xuan Zang
134	长孙皇后	Empress Zhangsun
136	武则天	Wu Zetian
138	狄仁杰	Di Renjie
140	慧能	Hui Neng
142	文成公主	Princess Wencheng
144	上官婉儿	Shangguan Wan'er
146	吴道子	Wu Daozi
148	鉴真	Jian Zhen
150	李白	Li Bai

152	王维	Wang Wei	202	晏几道	Yan Jidao	252	李时珍	Li Shizhen
154	颜真卿	Yan Zhenqing	204	黄庭坚	Huang Tingjian	254	冯小青	Feng Xiaoqing
156	杜甫	Du Fu	206	李清照	Li Qingzhao	256	李贽	Li Zhi
158	陆羽	Lu Yu	208	岳飞	Yue Fei	258	戚继光	Qi Jiguang
160	韩愈	Han Yu	210	陆游	Lu You	260	汤显祖	Tang Xianzu
162	刘禹锡	Liu Yuxi	212	张择端	Zhang Zeduan	262	徐光启	Xu Guangqi
164	王勃	Wang Bo	214	陆九渊	Lu Jiuyuan	264	冯梦龙	Feng Menglong
166	杨玉环	Yang Yuhuan	216	辛弃疾	Xin Qiji	266	徐霞客	Xu Xiake
168	白居易	Bai Juyi	218	赵佶	Zhao Ji	268	宋应星	Song Yingxing
170	董源	Dong Yuan	220	朱熹	Zhu Xi	270	史可法	Shi Kefa
172	柳宗元	Liu Zongyuan	222	关汉卿	Guan Hanqing	272	顾炎武	Gu Yanwu
174	赵匡胤	Zhao Kuangyin	224	郭守敬	Guo Shoujing	274	揭暄	Jie Xuan
176	乐史	Yue Shi	226	文天祥	Wen Tianxiang	276	柳如是	Liu Rushi
178	毕昇	Bi Sheng	228	黄道婆	Huang Daopo	278	郑成功	Zheng Chenggong
180	范仲淹	Fan Zhongyan	230	王实甫	Wang Shifu	280	梁章钜	Liang Zhangju
182	晏殊	Yan Shu	232	黄公望	Huang Gongwang	282	朱耷	Zhu Da
184	包拯	Bao Zheng	234	施耐庵	Shi Nai'an	284	龚自珍	Gong Zizhen
186	欧阳修	Ouyang Xiu	236	罗贯中	Luo Guanzhong	286	蒲松龄	Pu Songling
188	李觏	Li Gou	238	吴承恩	Wu Cheng'en	288	曹雪芹	Cao Xueqin
190	米芾	Mi Fu	240	朱元璋	Zhu Yuanzhang	290	石涛	Shi Tao
192	司马光	Sima Guang	242	郑和	Zheng He	292	郑板桥	Zheng Banqiao
194	曾巩	Zeng Gong	244	于谦	Yu Qian	294	林则徐	Lin Zexu
196	王安石	Wang Anshi	246	王守仁	Wang Shouren	296	魏源	Wei Yuan
198	沈括	Shen Kuo	248	王艮	Wang Gen	298	曾国藩	Zeng Guofan
200	苏轼	Su Shi	250	海瑞	Hai Rui	300	李鸿章	Li Hongzhang

中国古代 150 位历史名人画传 / ZHONGGUO GUDAI 150WEI LISHI MINGREN HUAZHUAN

引 言

Introduction

本书通过 150 幅历史人物画的精彩呈现，展示了中华民族在几千年的历史长河中生生不息、薪火相传、一脉相承的精神风貌：从三皇五帝、尧舜之治到皋陶断狱、仓颉造字；从孔孟论儒、老庄悟道到张骞出使、孙子用兵；从魏征进谏、海瑞上疏到文山正气、太祖礼贤；从子长著史、扬州尽忠到岳飞抗金、成功复台；从张衡制仪、仲景巡医到应星开物、冲之计数；从太白诗酒、东坡抒怀到张芝狂草、吴带当风；从鲁班传艺、道婆纺织到毕昇印刷、蔡伦造纸；从六祖坐禅、茶圣品茗到汉卿写戏、贯中撰书；从玄奘取经、郑和航海到则徐虎门销烟、海国图志……这些精彩的历史故事与鲜活的历史人物，借助于诗文、绘画来一一呈现，实是一幅浓缩了中华文明史的历史画卷。不仅让人们领略到历代先贤的伟大风范，而且让读者感悟到中华文明的博大精深。

This book aims to display the national spirit that Chinese people have handed down from generation to generation for centuries through a collection of biographies of 150 well-known figures in Chinese history. Readers will find many renowned historical figures and stories in this book covering diverse periods and areas, including The Three Sovereigns and Five Emperors, the great emperors Yao and Shun, China's first judge Gao Yao, the creator of Chinese characters Cangjie, the great philosophers Confucius, Mencius, Laozi and Zhuangzi, the trailblazer of the Silk Road Zhang Qian, the military strategist Sun Wu, the upright officials Wei Zheng and Hai Rui, the patriotic generals Wen Tianxiang, Yue Fei, Lin Zexu, Wei Yuan, and Zheng Chenggong, the distinguished poets Li Bai and Su Shi, the celebrated playwright Guan Hanqing, the brilliant novelist Luo Guanzhong, the eminent scientists Zhang Heng, Bi Sheng, and Cai Lun, the Buddhist scholar Xuanzang… the list goes on. We seek to bring Chinese history to life and present it to the readers vividly in the form of poetry and painting and in a way we see this book as a condensed presentation of Chinese civilization and history. We hope that readers will enjoy the charisma of these prominent people and the splendor of Chinese civilization through our efforts.

三皇五帝渺难寻，远古传来旷世音。
华夏文明由此始，张扬代代士人心。

The Three Sovereigns and Five Emperors 三皇五帝

　　三皇五帝，传说是原始社会中后期为人类做出卓越贡献的部落首领，后人追尊为"皇""帝"。

　　"三皇"：传为燧人氏（燧皇）、伏羲氏（羲皇）、神农氏（农皇）。燧皇属于石器时代，发明钻木取火，教会人们吃熟食，结束了茹毛饮血的历史；羲皇发明八卦，观察自然，预测天气变化，是人文之始；农皇又称炎帝，距今约五千五百年，发明耕作，开始种植，亲尝百草，为农业和中药之祖。五帝指黄帝、颛顼、帝喾、尧、舜，距今四千余年。黄帝时期发明文字，记事开始；颛顼时期发明制铜，进行工具改革；帝喾时期，发现节令，指导农时；尧时开始制定规矩；舜时开始分工管理。

　　以上"皇""帝"均是大爱大公的领袖。"炎黄"是炎帝、黄帝的缩写，"炎黄子孙"的称谓即来源于此，"炎黄子孙"已成为华夏儿女的代称。

三皇五帝

[唐] 杨简

混沌凿开吞几岁，洪荒莫考传承裔。
但闻前史载三皇，伏义神农及黄帝。
三皇之后五帝传，少昊颛顼高辛继。
唐尧虞舜又继之，天下于斯为盛际。

The Three Sovereigns and Five Emperors were a group of mythological tribal leaders in ancient China. They were given the titles of "sovereign" and "emperor" because of their significant contributions to mankind.

The Three Sovereigns supposedly comprise of Suiren-shi (The Sui Sovereign), Fuxi-shi (The Xi Sovereign) and Shennong-shi (The Nong Sovereign). The Sui Sovereign lived in the Stone Age. He taught people to drill wood to make fire and eat cooked food. The Xi Sovereign, besides inventing Bagua, observed the nature and forecasted the weather. He was credited with creating humanity. The Nong Sovereign, also called Yandi, lived 5,500 years ago. He first taught people the practices of agriculture and is said to have tasted hundreds of herbs to ascertain their qualities. He is thus regarded as the father of agriculture and Chinese medicine.

The Five Emperors comprise of Huangdi (the Yellow Emperor), Emperor Zhuanxu, Emperor Ku, Emperor Yao, and Emperor Shun, who lived about 4,000 years ago. Huangdi created the first Chinese character writing system and enabled people to start recording history. In the reign of Zhuanxu, the ancient Chinese started mining and making tools out of bronze. In Emperor Ku's reign, the 24 solar terms were discovered and provided a time frame for agriculture. Emperor Yao started the rule of law and Emperor Shun governed the country by implementing clear division of work.

The Three Sovereigns and Five Emperors were all benevolent rulers. The Chinese people later coined the term "Yanhuang" (a combination of "Yandi" and "Huangdi") and called themselves "the descendants of Yanhuang".

三皇五帝图

Nüwa 女娲

闻说天崩地裂时，先民水火兽禽欺。
女神熔石补亏缺，一曲九州生态诗。

吹笙引

[唐] 王毂

娲皇遗音寄玉笙，双成传得何凄清。
丹穴娇雏七十只，一时飞上秋天鸣。
水泉迸泻急相续，一束宫商裂寒玉。
旖旎香风绕指生，千声妙尽神仙曲。
曲终满席悄无语，巫山冷碧愁云雨。

　　女娲，亦称娲皇、帝娲、风皇、女皇等，《史记》称女娲氏，风（或为凤、女）姓，是古代传说中的大地之母。相传她是华夏族的母亲，她慈祥地创造了生命，又勇敢地照顾生灵免受天灾，是被民间广泛而又长久崇拜的创世神和始母神。她神通广大，能化生万物，每天至少能创造出七十样东西。传说女娲用黄土仿照自己造人，创造了人类社会。还有传说当时自然界发生了一场特大灾害，天塌地陷，猛禽恶兽都出来残害百姓，女娲熔炼五色石来修补苍天，又杀死恶兽猛禽，重立四极天柱，平整天地。记载中她替人类建立了婚姻制度，使青年两性相互婚配、繁衍后代，因此也被传为婚姻女神。

Nüwa, also known as Empress Wa, was the mother of earth in Chinese mythology. Legend sees her as the mother of the Chinese people, who created mankind and protected them from natural disasters. Nüwa was widely regarded as the mother goddess and the goddess of creation in ancient China. Being very mighty, Nüwa could supposedly create 70 things in a day. She was also credited with creating human beings by molding figures from the yellow earth and giving them life, thus creating human societies. When the heavens collapsed and the earth caved in, and birds of prey and fierce beasts appeared to destroy mankind, she melted five-colored stones to patch up the sky, killed the birds and beasts, and restored the four pillars that supported the heavens. Nüwa also established the norms for marriage and reproduction and was therefore also known as the goddess of martial affairs.

女娲补天图

Yao 唐 尧

唐尧修政恤饥贫，圣德如天无怨民。
凿井耕田皆自乐，相交处事有遵循。

谒尧帝庙

[唐] 轩辕弥明

祖龙开国尽遐荒，庙建唐尧镇此邦。
山卷白云朝帝座，林疏红日列仙幢。
巍巍圣迹陵松峤，荡荡恩波洽桂江。
瞻仰威灵共回首，紫霞深处锁轩窗。

　　尧为帝喾之子，受封于唐地（今山西太原），故又称唐尧。唐尧时期定历法，典三礼，明五刑，民有遵循，使人类进入有序社会。尧关注百姓疾苦，重视民生，设谏言之鼓，立诽谤之木，让百姓参与政事，因而政治清明。据《帝王本纪》记载，帝尧之世，天下大和，百姓无事。
　　尧后来将帝位禅让于舜。

Yao was the son of Emperor Ku. He was made ruler of the Tang region (now Taiyuan, Shanxi) so was also known as Tang Yao. Yao was credited with bringing order to the human society by designing the traditional Chinese calendar and enacting clear laws. He was also noted for his benevolence and orderly governance of the country. He passed his throne to Shun after he abdicated.

/ 中国古代150位历史名人画传 /
ZHONGGUO GUDAI 150WEI LISHI MINGREN HUAZHUAN

唐尧圣德图

Shun 虞舜

虞舜孝行天下闻,父盲母劣弟难群。
能将德惠平私怨,是以成名有道君。

舜庙怀古
[宋]陆游

云断苍梧竟不归,江边古庙锁朱扉。
山川不为兴亡改,风月应怜感慨非。
孤枕有时莺唤梦,斜风无赖客添衣。
千年回首消磨尽,输与渔舟送落晖。

  舜的父亲失明,继母无德,弟弟顽劣(继母所生)。舜从小受继母虐待,多次被继母和弟弟迫害,仍和善相对,以德报怨,以孝行闻名。又办事公正,才干突出。尧把娥皇、女英两个女儿配为舜妻,后又将帝位禅让给舜。舜继位,巡行天下,四海咸服。又明确九官职责,如大禹治水、皋陶掌刑等,三年一考核,致天下大治。舜后来将帝位禅让给禹。

  Shun's mother died when he was young and his father, who was blind, remarried after Shun's mother's death. Shun's stepmother and half-brother treated Shun badly but Shun always treated them with kindness. Shun was famous for his filial piety, integrity and leadership skills and Emperor Yao married his two daughters to him and finally appointed him as the heir to the throne. After ascending to the throne, Shun toured the entire country and was admired by the people. He ruled the country by appointing officials with clear division of work and assessed them every three years, which turned out to be effective and put all national affairs in proper order. When he abdicated, Shun passed the throne to Yu.

虞舜禅让图

Yu 夏禹

禹王治水九州平，疏导箴言天地情。
治水安邦原一理，惜其身后有违卿。

夏禹
[宋]王十朋

洪流浩浩浸寰区，民杂蛇龙鸟兽居。
长叹当时微帝力，苍生今日尽为鱼。

　　禹开启了夏朝历史，因此后人称他为夏禹。夏禹最卓著的功绩是改革治水方法，将"堵"的方法改为"疏"，令黄河水患平息，民生得以安定。夏禹并划定中国版图为九州，团结部落首领，教化少数民族，建立了中国历史上第一个王朝，使中国社会进入奴隶社会。夏禹逝世后，他的儿子启继承了王位，终结了禅让制，开始了世袭制。

Yu was said to have established the Xia dynasty so was also called Xia Yu by Chinese people. Xia Yu was best known for improving the system to control flooding. Instead of directly damming the floods' flow, Yu built many canals which relieved floodwater into fields and the ocean. Yu divided China into nine provinces, united all tribes and minority groups and built the first dynasty in Chinese history. It also initiated ancient China's history of slavery. After his death, Yu's son succeeded to the throne. Thereafter, the abdication system was replaced by the hereditary system.

大禹治水图

Gao Yao 皋陶

刑法皋陶称始祖，先行教化后惩身。
世间贪欲如洪水，警戒原来是爱民。

过皋陶庙
[明] 于谦

明刑弼教佐雍熙，千载嘉谟仰士师。
故里凄凉遗旧塚，穹碑剥落倚荒祠。
虞廷法立人无犯，后世民生为益滋。
庙貌幸存神未泯，赓歌犹得想当时。

　　皋陶，虞舜和夏禹时期的一位贤臣，是与尧、舜、禹齐名的"上古四贤"。皋陶多才，是上古时期杰出的政治家、思想家和教育家，是被史学界和司法界公认的中国司法鼻祖。

　　皋陶的主要功绩是从爱民利民出发，推行"刑教兼施"策略，颁"五刑"、立"五教"，将"法治"与"德治"相结合；并"画地为牢"，初设监狱，以改造违法者。皋陶明察秋毫，办案公正，断案如神。

Gao Yao was a prominent statesman, thinker and educationist during the reign of Shun and Yu. He was considered one of the "Four Sages of ancient China" along with Yao, Shun and Yu, and was revered as the creator of the earliest judicial system of China.

Gao Yao created China's earliest criminal law in order to protect the people. He also established China's earliest prison for rehabilitating criminals. Besides, he was widely acclaimed as an impartial and competent judge.

皋陶司法图

Cang Jie 仓　颉

汉字之初图物形，因将木石刻于铭。
纷繁世事难应对，遂有六书传六经。

望仓颉墓

［明］曾省吾

仓圣前村古墓扃，千峰雨气昼冥冥。
鬼声龙影藏何处，丹甲青文想巨灵。
元化本从秦地辟，精魂应识楚人经。
乞将心画传诸子，鹑首行占聚五星。

　　仓颉，黄帝的助手，传说任史官，负责记录事件而造文字。
　　仓颉仰观天象，俯察地理及动物形貌爪痕，受到启迪，根据事物形状创造了象形文字。他广泛搜集民间刻在竹木石头上的象形图，整理出一套象形文字，结束了结绳、积木、堆石等原始记事方式，被尊为"造字圣人"。

Cangjie was supposedly the official historian of the Yellow Emperor. He was in charge of recording information and was credited with inventing Chinese characters.
Legend has it that Cangjie was inspired by an impression of a hoof-print and created a character writing system by capturing the appearances and characteristics of objects. His creation replaced the old record keeping method that used ropes, woods and stones. Cangjie was revered as "the saint of characters".

仓颉造字图

Du Kang 杜 康

杜康何故造奇方，遂令江山几许狂。
醉客三千天地乍，豪强数盏上山梁。

酒诰

[西晋] 江统

酒之所兴，肇自上皇；
或云仪狄，一曰杜康。
有饭不尽，委余空桑；
郁积成味，久蓄气芳。
本出于此，不由奇方。

　　杜康，又名少康，夏朝人，酿酒师。传说杜康为粮食保管员，偶然机会见粮食发酵，遂发明造酒，后世尊奉他为制酒业的祖师爷、"酒圣"，"杜康"也成了美酒的代名词。

　　"何以解忧？唯有杜康"。酒使生活增添色彩，让社会增加热度。庆典祭祀、交友酬宾少不了酒；煮酒论英雄，杯酒释兵权……历史事件偶然间因酒而改变过目，这一切都离不开杜康的贡献。

Du Kang, also called Shao Kang, lived in the Xia dynasty. Legend has it that Du was a granary official and once saw fermented millet by chance. Inspired by the discovery, he began to produce and sell alcohol. Du is revered as the founder of the winemaking industry in China and people often use his name "Du Kang" to refer to any good alcohol.

Cao Cao, a famous Chinese general and poet once wrote "How can I dissolve my woes? It's only through Du Kang's brew." Wine drinking is an important part of Chinese culture, and has even influenced many historical events. This would not have been possible if it weren't for Du Kang.

杜康酿酒图

Yi Yin 伊 尹

蓄意厨师做嫁奴,幸而明主识君殊。
调和五味知施政,火候高低名实符。

秋日偶成(摘录)
[宋] 程颢

圣贤事业本经纶,肯为巢由继后尘。
三币未回伊尹志,万钟难换子舆贫。

伊尹,名伊,一说名挚,夏末商初人,政治家、思想家,厨师。

传伊尹生于伊水旁(河南),故以伊为氏,后流落耕于有莘之野,被有莘(陕西)国君庖人收养。伊尹虽为奴,而乐尧舜之道,好究前代治理得失。得遇商汤,伊尹以烹调之理说治理之道,得商汤赏识,任为尹(相),佐汤灭夏。伊尹主持治理50年,先后经五位君主,兢兢业业,在政治、军事、文化、教育等多方面有建树,令商代经济繁荣,国力强盛。其"调和五味""火候论"的烹调理论用以治国,正合老子的"治大国若烹小鲜",后世称之为帝王之师、中华厨祖,成为中国历史上第一位贤相。

Yi Yin was a famous politician, thinker and cook in ancient China. He lived in the late Xia and early Shang dynasties.

Legend has it that Yi was born at the bank of the Yi River in Henan and therefore bore the surname Yi. Born as a slave, Yi was later adopted by an imperial cook of the State of Shen. Gifted in both cooking and political affairs, he later became the chef of Tang, the Emperor of the Shang dynasty, and advised the emperor on state affairs while serving him. Impressed by his talents, Tang appointed him as "Yin" (prime minster). Yi later helped Tang defeat the Xia dynasty and held the post of prime minster for 50 years, during which he served five emperors successively. While he was in office, Yi worked conscientiously and made outstanding contributions in politics, military training, culture, education, etc. and brought Shang to a new level of prosperity. Yi was noted for comparing the governing of a state to the cooking of a delicious dish, and was revered as the founder of Chinese cooking and the first outstanding prime minister in Chinese history.

厨祖伊尹图

Ji Chang 姬 昌

慎刑明德文王始,广聚贤才礼乐兴。
羑里城中演周易,千秋理政为准绳。

周易(节选)
[周] 姬昌

天行健,君子以自强不息,
地势坤,君子以厚德载物。

　　姬昌(公元前1152年—公元前1056年),姬姓,名昌,周太王之孙,季历之子,周朝奠基者,岐周(今陕西岐山)人。其父死后,继承西伯侯之位,故称西伯昌。西伯昌四十二年,姬昌称王,史称周文王。

　　姬昌勤于政事,重视发展农业生产,礼贤下士,广罗人才,拜姜尚为军师,问以军国大计,使"天下三分,其二归周";收复虞、芮两国,攻灭黎(今山西长治)、邘(今河南沁阳)等国;建都丰京(今陕西西安),为武王灭商奠基;创周礼,被后世儒家所推崇。姬昌生活勤俭,穿普通人的衣服,还到田间劳动,兢兢业业治理周朝。周朝在他的治理下,国力日渐强大。在位50年,是中国历史上的一代明君。

Ji Chang (1152—1056 BC), a native of Qizhou (now Qishan, Shaanxi), was the grandson of the Grand Duke and son of King Ji of the State of Zhou. He was also known as the founder of the Zhou dynasty. After his father deceased, Ji inherited the title of Duke Xibo, thus was also referred to as Xibo Chang. Ji later ascended to the throne and became the King Wen of Zhou.

Ji handled political affairs diligently and attached much importance to agricultural production. He was courteous to the scholars and recruited talents readily. He appointed Jiang Shang as military counsellor and consulted him about state affairs. He later conquered the States of Yu, Rui, Li (now Changzhi, Shanxi), Yu (now Qinyang, Henan), etc., set Fengjing (now Xi'an, Shaanxi) as the capital, and paved the way for his successor, King Wu of Zhou, to defeat the Shang dynasty. The rituals he created for Zhou were highly praised by the Confucianists in later generations. Ji was noted for living a frugal life as a king. Legend has it that he would wear commoners' clothing and take up farming in the fields. He ruled the state meticulously and raised Zhou gradually to prosperity. He reigned for a total of 50 years and was revered as an outstanding, virtuous king in Chinese history.

姬昌纳贤图

Jiang Shang 姜 尚

飘蓬半世几浮沉,欲展雄才报国门。
渭水直钩何自信?原知明主重贤人。

留别于十一兄逖裴十三游塞垣
[唐] 李白

太公渭川水,李斯上蔡门。
钓周猎秦安黎元,小鱼兔兔何足言?
天张云卷有时节,吾徒莫叹羝触藩。
于公白首大梁野,使人怅望何可论?
即知朱亥为壮士,且愿束心秋毫里。
秦赵虎争血中原,当去抱关救公子。
裴生览千古,龙鸾炳天章。
悲吟雨雪动林木,放书辍剑思高堂。
劝尔一杯酒,拂尔裘上霜。
尔为我楚舞,吾为尔楚歌。
且探虎穴向沙漠,鸣鞭走马凌黄河。
耻作易水别,临歧泪滂沱。

姜尚(公元前 1156 年—公元前 1017 年),字子牙,商末周初政治家、军事家。

姜尚先辈辅佐夏禹治水有功,封吕,故姓吕,又名望,生于没落家族,当过屠夫,开过酒店,虽落魄而好学不倦,博学多闻。曾为商纣王小吏,不被重用,游说诸侯,未得赏识。老年闻说西伯侯重贤,遂潜隐其境,70 多岁时垂钓渭水之滨,遇到求贤若渴的姬昌(即后来的周文王)。文王拜姜尚为师,姜尚辅助文王兴周。姜尚仍为相国,同政治家姬旦(周公旦)一同辅助武王打败商纣王,取得天下,建立周朝。姜尚受封于齐国(都城在今山东淄博),为齐国开国君主。

Jiang Shang (1156 —1017 BC), also known as Jiang Ziya, was a statesman and military strategist of the late Shang and early Zhou dynasties.

Jiang Shang's ancestors once helped Yu (the leader of Xia) to control floods, and were conferred with the surname Lü. Thus, he was also less often known as Lü Wang. Born in a declining family, he once worked as a butcher and inn keeper. Despite the deprived life, Jiang studied hard and acquired extensive knowledge. He once served as a minor official under King Zhou of Shang, but his talents were not appreciated when he tried advising the state rulers. Jiang later learned that King Wen of Zhou desired talented advisors. He then went angling at the Weishui River to get his attention. He angled in a bizarre way, using a straight hook without bait, on the theory that the fish would come to him of their own volition when they were ready, and was eventually appointed as King Wen's teacher and advisor. Along with statesman Ji Dan, Jiang helped King Wen and his son King Wu overthrow the Shang dynasty and establish the Zhou dynasty. Jiang was later awarded the Qi region (now Shandong) for his contributions.

太公垂钓图

Li Er 李 耳

道德真经日月光，世情参透辨阴阳。
无为小吏成奇器，大智五千东土芳。

不尚贤，使民不争；不贵难得之货，使民不为盗；不见可欲，使民心不乱。是以圣人之治，虚其心，实其腹，弱其志，强其骨。常使民无知无欲。使夫智者不敢为也。为无为，则无不治。

——［春秋］老 子

李耳（公元前571年—公元前471年），又称老聃，字伯阳，世称老子。春秋时期楚国苦县（今河南鹿邑）人，哲学家、思想家，道家学派创始人。

曾在太学就学研究，后为周室守藏室史（掌管图书等经典物件）多年，勤奋钻研，因周室衰弱而日月苦思，悟出道，著有《道德经》八十一章共五千字。主张道为万物之源，遵从客观，崇尚无为，又主张事物对应变化的朴素唯物辩证法则。其学说对中国哲学思想影响深远，孔子曾向老子请教，有"老子天下第一"之说，被誉为东方三大圣人之首，列为世界文化名人，"世界古今十大作家"之首。

Li Er (571—471 BC), better known as Laozi or Laodan, was a native of the State of Chu (now Henan) of the Spring and Autumn Period. He was a philosopher, thinker and the founder of Taoism
Li once studied at the imperial college and worked as an archivist at the Imperial Library of the Zhou Court. He contemplated about philosophy for years and turned his thoughts into the work *Tao Te Ching*, containing 5,000 characters and 81 chapters. He held the view that the Tao is the source of all things and people should obey the laws of nature. He advocated the concept of wu wei, meaning "non-action" or "doing nothing" and believed in dialectical materialism. Li's doctrine has a far-reaching influence on Chinese philosophy. He was venerated by Confucius as the greatest person ever and had a worldwide reputation as a philosopher.

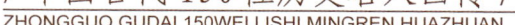

老子悟道图

Wu Yuan 伍 员

为报亲仇两鬓斑，成吴霸业气如山。
赴汤蹈火曾无敌，怎奈忠良自理难。

伍子胥庙
[宋] 王禹偁

朝驱下越坂，夕饮当吴门。
停车访古迹，霭霭林烟昏。
青山海上来，势若游龙奔。
星临斗牛卷，气与东南吞。
九折排怒涛，壮哉天地垠。
落日见海色，长风卷浮云。
山椒戴遗祠，兴废今犹存。
残香吊木客，倒树哀清猿。
我来久沉抱，重此英烈魂。
嗟吁属镂锋，冥尔国士冤。
峨峨姑苏台，榛棘晚露繁。
深居麋鹿游，此事谁能论。
因之毛发竖，落叶秋纷纷。

伍员（公元前559年—公元前484年），字子胥，春秋时期楚国（湖北省监利，一说安徽省全椒）人，政治家、军事家。

伍子胥之父伍奢和兄伍尚因受谗言，被楚平王杀害。伍子胥从楚国逃到吴国，成为吴国重臣，辅助吴王富国强兵，协同孙武打败楚国，报了亲仇。吴国打败越国等国后，成为诸侯霸主，伍员建议灭掉越国，而吴王夫差反而听信谗言赐伍员宝剑，令其自裁，忠良不保。

传说伍员当年为逃出楚境伺机报仇，因难过昭关而一夜愁白了头。

Wu Yuan (559—484 BC), also called Wu Zixu, was a native of the State of Chu (now Jianli, Hubei or Quanjiao, Anhui). He was a statesman and military strategist of the Spring and Autumn Period.

Wu's father Wu She and brother Wu Shang were slandered and falsely killed by King Ping of Chu. Wu, promising revenge, fled to the State of Wu and became a trusted advisor there. He, along with Sun Wu, helped build up Wu's national strength and finally defeated Chu and revenged his father and brother. Wu then suggested King Fuchai to overthrow the State of Yue, but was slandered by other officials and forced to commit suicide.

According to legend, under enormous stress, Wu's hair turned completely white overnight at Zhaoguan pass in the process of his escape.

伍员复国图

Lu Ban 鲁　班

巧匠能工自鲁班，行居食用解难关。
凡人借得神仙力，智慧长存岁月间。

扶风歌
[晋] 刘琨

南山石嵬嵬，松柏何离离。
上枝拂青云，中心十数围。
洛阳发中梁，松树窃自悲。
斧锯截是松，松树东西摧。
特作四轮车，载至洛阳宫。
观者莫不叹，问是何山材。
谁能刻镂此，公输与鲁班。
被之用丹漆，熏用苏合香。
本自南山松，今为宫殿梁。

鲁班（公元前507年—公元前444年），春秋时期鲁国人，姬姓，公输氏，名班，人称公输盘、公输般、班输，尊称公输子，惯称"鲁班"。大约在公元前450年以后，他从鲁国来到楚国，帮助楚国制造兵器。他曾创制云梯，准备攻宋国，墨子不远千里，从鲁行十日十夜至楚国都城郢，与鲁班和楚王相互辩难，强行说服楚王停止攻宋。

鲁班的名字实际上已经成为古代劳动人民智慧的象征。人们把古代劳动人民的集体创造和发明也都集中到他的身上。木工师傅们用的手工工具，如钻、刨子、铲子、曲尺，划线用的墨斗，据说都是鲁班发明的。有关他的发明和创造的故事，实际上是中国古代劳动人民发明创造的故事。

Lu Ban (507—444 BC), also known as Gongshu Ban, was born in the State of Lu during the Spring and Autumn Period. He was a Chinese carpenter, engineer and inventor during the Zhou dynasty.

After 450 B.C., he left the State of Lu and came to the State of Chu. He started to manufacture weapons for the State of Chu. He once ingeniously created cloud ladder to help the state of Chu to attack the State of Song. Mo Zi departed from the State of Lu, took ten days and ten nights to arrive at Ying (the capital city of the State of Chu). He argued with Lu Ban and King of Chu, forcibly persuaded King of Chu out of attacking the State of Song. The name Lu Ban has actually become the symbol of all labor people's wisdom in ancient times. People have concentrated the collective creations and inventions of the ancient working people on him. It is said that he has invented or improved a number of carpenter's tools—the saw, the square, the planer, the drill, the shovel, and an ink marking tool etc. The story about his invention and creation is actually the story of the invention and creation of the working people in ancient China.

鲁班授徒图

Confucius 孔子

仁义礼智圣贤书,世乱宏才未展舒。
是以经纶昭弟子,独尊儒术汉时初。

学而时习之,不亦说乎?有朋自远方来,不亦乐乎?人不知而不愠,不亦君子乎?

——[春秋]孔子

孔子（公元前551年—公元前479年），名丘，字仲尼，春秋末期生于鲁国陬邑（今属山东曲阜），思想家、教育家，儒家学派的创始人。

孔子任过鲁国大司寇，管理司法（时间较短），一生主要的业绩是开门授徒，开创了私人讲学之风。相传有弟子三千，其中贤人七十二。孔子带领弟子周游列国，晚年组织修订"六经"：《诗》《书》《礼》《乐》《易》《春秋》。孔子去世后，其弟子及其再传弟子把孔子及其弟子的言行记录下来，整理后编成儒家经典《论语》。汉武帝"罢黜百家，独尊儒术"，孔子被尊为圣人，后世历代王朝均以追封，号"万世师表"。其儒家思想对中国和世界都有深远的影响，被列为"世界十大文化名人"。

Confucius (551 – 479 BC), also named Qiu or Zhongni, was born in the Zou District in the state of Lu (now Qufu, Shandong) in the late Spring and Autumn Period. He was one of the greatest thinkers and educators in Chinese history and the founder of Confucianism.

Confucius once served as the Dasikou (manager of criminals) in the state of Lu and was in charge of judicial affairs. He was celebrated for his outstanding contributions in education. He was thought to be the first teacher in Chinese history and the progenitor of the vocation of teaching. It was believed that Confucius had a total of 3,000 students, and 72 of them mastered the "six arts". He once journeyed across many states with his students and, in his later years, he led the compilation of the "Six Classics", which comprised *Shi* (The Book of Songs), *Shu* (Collection of Ancient Texts), *Li* (Records of Rites), *Yue* (The Book on Music), *Yi* (The Book of Changes), and *Chun Qiu* (The Spring and Autumn Annals). After his death, Confucius's students compiled his teachings into *The Analects of Confucius*, an all-time Confucian classic. During the succeeding Han dynasty, Confucianism was set as the orthodox imperial philosophy, and Confucius was revered as a saint. He also gained sustained and widespread prominence in varied dynasties throughout Chinese history and was acclaimed as "the paragon of teachers for ten thousand generations". With a profound and far-reaching impact in China and overseas, Confucius has been selected as the world's top ten cultural celebrities.

孔子授课图

Sun Wu 孙 武

军为国事孰能轻，胜负先应决策明。
奇正虚赢因势变，兵书岂止在言兵。

> 胜不过众人之所知，非善之善者也；战胜而天下曰善，非善之善者也。
> ——［春秋］孙 子

孙武（公元前 545 年—公元前 470 年），春秋末期齐国乐安（今山东广饶）人，军事家、政治家。

著有《孙子兵法》13 篇 6000 字，是中国现存最早的兵书，孙武被后人誉为"兵圣"。其兵法被翻译成英、法、德、日等多国文字，成为风行世界的兵书典范。《孙子兵法》阐述了战争中制胜的规律、战略原则、临阵战术及军队的后勤保障等，内容丰富，文字精炼。书中强调战争中的主观能动性及应对客观之道，充满辩证法，其基本原则被后人广泛应用于社会、经济各方面。

Sun Wu (545 – 470 BC), also known as Sunzi, was a native of Le'an of the State of Qi (now Guangrao, Shandong). He was a prominent military strategist and statesman of the late Spring and Autumn Period.

Sun was most famous for his work *The Art of War*, which, comprising 13 chapters and 6,000 Chinese characters, is China's oldest extant work on military affairs. Sun was revered as the "Saint of Military" by later generations for this masterpiece. *The Art of War* has been translated into many languages including English, French, Germany, and Japanese, and has gained worldwide prestige. It covers a wide range of topics on warfare including grand strategy, tactics, logistics, etc., and is thought to have embodied dialectical thinking. Sun's principles of warfare have been applied in the economy and many other areas of society.

孙子著兵书图

Fan Li 范 蠡

兴越良谋称范蠡，功成退隐五湖中。
陶朱首富尊齐鲁，可见商情政理通。

飞鸟尽，良弓藏；狡兔死，
走狗烹。
——［春秋］范 蠡

　　范蠡（公元前536年—公元前448年），字少伯，春秋末期楚国宛地（今河南南阳）人，政治家、实业家。

　　范蠡扶助越王勾践兴国称霸后及时隐退，泛舟五湖，遨游于七十二峰之间。后居于定陶（今山东菏泽市定陶区）经商，自号陶朱公，成齐鲁首富。又三散家财以自守，被后人尊称为"商圣"。

　　范蠡洞察时势，据时而动，进退自如，得失均衡，既有治国之雄才，又有经商之大略，政商兼通，实为历史上罕见的智谋奇士。

Fan Li (536—448 BC), courtesy name Shaobo, a native of Wan region in the State of Chu (now Nanyang, Henan), was a prominent statesman and industrialist in the late Spring and Autumn Period.

After Fan Li helped Goujian to win a decisive victory for the State of Yue over the State of Wu, he retired to live a secluded life on a fishing boat, roaming the misty wilderness of Lake Tai and various mountains. Later, he settled down in Dingtao (now Dingtao District in Heze, Shandong) to take up business. He is also known by the name Tao Zhu Gong as the wealthiest citizen in the land of Qilu. He once became extremely wealthy for three times, and each time gave away everything he had. He was praised as the Saint of Business by later generations.

As an important political and military advisor as well as the founding father of Chinese commercial business, Fan Li can be said to be the prominent talent rare to be seen throughout the history.

范蠡兴越图

Xi Shi 西 施

浣纱少女本幽闲，为惑吴王出越关。
相惜心中无限意，俗情消逝宦情间。

西 施
［唐］罗隐

家国兴亡自有时，
吴人何苦怨西施。
西施若解倾吴国，
越国亡来又是谁？

　　西施，本名施夷光。春秋末年越国美女（今浙江诸暨苎萝村人氏），又称"西子"。

　　当时越国称臣于吴国，越王勾践卧薪尝胆，谋求复国。国难当头之际，西施忍辱负重，曲线救国，她与郑旦一起被越王勾践献给吴王，成为吴王最宠爱的妃子，把吴王迷惑得众叛亲离，无心国事，为勾践的东山再起起到了举足轻重的作用，表现出高尚的情操和爱国情怀。后吴国终被越国所灭。

　　传说越国灭吴后，西施与范蠡泛舟五湖，不知所终，备受后人景仰。

Xi Shi, also known as Shi Yiguang or Lady Xi, was a native of the present-day Zhuluo Village, Zhuji in Zhejiang province. She was a renowned beauty in the State of Yue in the late Spring and Autumn Period.

For the imminent national crisis, Xishi decided to save the State of Yue by a devious path. King Goujian of Yue was once imprisoned by King Fuchai of Wu after a defeat in war, and Yue later became a tributary state to Wu. Xi Shi was offered to King Fuchai of Wu by Goujian as a tribute along with Zheng Dan. She became the most favored concubine of King Fuchai of Wu. Bewitched by the beauty and kindness of Xi Shi, Fuchai forgot all about his state affairs and killed his best advisor Wu Zixu. She played a vital role in the resurgence of Goujian and manifested noble sentiments and patriotism. Later, the state of Wu was finally overthrown by the State of Yue.

In the legend, after the fall of Wu, Fan Li retired from his ministerial post and lived with Xi Shi on a fishing boat, roaming like fairies in the misty wilderness of Lake Tai, and no one saw them ever again. Both of them were revered by later generations.

西施浣纱图

Gou Jian 勾践

越王无愧禹王孙，尝胆朝朝夕卧薪。
苦役三年终霸业，能申能屈属斯人。

越王勾践墓

[宋] 柴望

秦望山头自夕阳，伤心谁复赋凄凉？
今人不见亡吴事，故墓犹传霸越乡。
雨打乱花迷复道，鸟翻黄叶下宫墙。
登临莫向高台望，烟树中原正渺茫。

　　勾践（公元前520年—公元前465年），夏禹后裔，春秋末年越国国君。因败于吴国，沦为吴国臣仆，为吴王养马。三年中谦恭勤勉，备尝艰辛，吴王赦免。勾践害怕自己会因贪图眼前的安逸而丧失报国雪耻之志，他为自己安排艰苦的生活环境，晚上睡觉不用被褥，只铺柴草；又在屋里挂了一只苦胆，不时尝尝苦胆的味道，为的是不忘过去的耻辱。勾践重用范蠡、文种等忠良人才，吸取教训，历十余年，国力大增。励志兴国报仇，为鼓励民众，勾践和王后参与劳动，在越人同心协力之下，越国逐渐强大起来。后终于大败吴师，灭吴国而称霸。

Goujian (520—465 BC) was the King of Yue during the Spring and Autumn Period. In his reign, Yue was defeated by Wu and Goujian was captured and served as a servant of the King of Wu for three years before he was released and returned to his state. Goujian aspired to seek revenge. He was known for forcing himself to sleep on sticks and taste bile in order to remember his humiliations while being held hostage in Wu. He appointed skilled politicians, such as Fan Li and Wen Zhong, to help rule the kingdom. After ten years of reform, Yue became much stronger and defeated Wu.

勾践卧薪尝胆图

Mo Di 墨 翟

贫苦小民成大贤，尚同兼爱道空前。
非攻节用求平等，后世几人能比肩。

> 夫爱人者，人必从而爱之；利人者，人必从而利之；恶人者，人必从而恶之；害人者，人必从而害之。
>
> ——[春秋] 墨 子

墨子（公元前468年—公元前376年），名翟，春秋末战国初鲁国人，出生于今山东滕州市，思想家、教育家、军事家，墨家学派的创始人。

墨子出身底层，精通手工艺。初曾从师于儒者，学习孔子之术，后来不满儒家"礼"的烦琐，舍弃儒学，另立新说，形成了自己的墨家学派，成为儒家的主要对立派，是先秦时代唯一能与儒家学派相抗衡的"世之显学"。墨子主张尚同、尚贤、兼爱、非攻，非乐节用等。生活上奉行"以自苦为极"，甘于清贫，乐于奉献。这些思想代表了平民意愿，其学说属于平民哲学。

《墨子》53篇，由其门徒增补而成，内容广博，包括了政治军事、哲学伦理、逻辑及自然科学技术之天文学、几何光学、静力学等方面。

Mo Di (468—376 BC), a native of the State of Lu in Late Spring and Autumn Period and the early Warring States Period. Born in the present-day Tengzhou, Shandong, he was a thinker, educator, military strategist as well as the founder of Mo School.

Mo Di was born in an underclass family and was skilled in craftsmanship. Mo Di was originally a follower of the teachings of Confucius, until he became convinced that Confucianism laid too much emphasis on a burdensome code of rituals and too little on religious teaching, at which time Mo Di decided to go his own way and finally evolved a doctrine of universal love that gave rise to a religious movement called Mohism. Mo School became the main opposition school of Confucianism and was the only "scientific study" that could compete with the Confucian school in the pre-Qin period.

Mo Zi upheld the following tenets: exaltation of the virtuous, identification with the superior, universal love, condemnation of offensive war, economy of expenditures, denunciation of music as a wasteful activity etc. He was contented in poverty with the spirit of dedication. His thoughts reflected the commoners' aspirations and his doctrine belongs to commoners' philosophy.

The contents of *Mo Di* (53 articles) was supplemented and complied by his disciples. This book has abundant contents including political military, philosophical ethics, logic and natural science and technology (in aspect of astronomy, geometrical optics and statics etc.)

墨翟甘于清贫图

Shang Yang 商 鞅

严明法治始商鞅，重本废封秦国强。
自古革新多阻碍，刑场就义几人伤？

> 圣人知治国之要，故令民归心于农。圣人为民法，必使之明白易知，愚智遍在之。
>
> 圣人为国也，观俗立法则治，察国事本则宜。
>
> ——［战国］商 鞅

　　商鞅（约公元前395年—公元前338年），战国时期卫国（今河南安阳）人，政治家，著名法家学派的代表人物。

　　商鞅是卫国国君的后裔，本为卫鞅，后封于商，故称商鞅。商鞅年轻时好刑名之学，钻研以法治理，先在魏国，但未得重用，闻秦孝公下令求贤，乃离魏去秦。在秦主持军政大权19年，先后两次推行变法，废井田、开阡陌，实行郡县制，奖励军功，重视耕织，实行连坐之法。秦得以国富民强兵勇。孝公去世后，太子秦惠王继位，贵族诬告商鞅有谋反企图，被车裂、灭族。而其变法措施继续执行，国事民生照旧。著有《商君书》，内容是变法措施的诠释。

Shang Yang (about 395—338 BC), a native of the State of Wei (now Anyang, Henan), was a statesman and a representative figure of Legalist School in the Warring States Period.

Shang Yang was born in an aristocrat family in the State of Wei. When he was young, he was interested in laws and made in-depth research in law-based governance. With the support of Duke Xiao of Qin, Shang Yang left his lowly position in Wei to become the chief adviser in Qin. He has held major military and political powers in the State of Qin for nineteen years. He introduced two political reforms to the State of Qin to establish the political system of prefecture and county to abolish the nine-square system and make land private, and implement collective punishment procedure. He instituted compulsory military service and a new system of land division and taxation and insisted on strict and uniform administration of the law. His numerous reforms transformed the peripheral Qin state into a militarily powerful and strongly centralized kingdom. When he fell into disgrace for the reason of other's slander, he was tied to chariots and torn apart. Moreover, his whole family was also executed. Relevant measures on his political reform were continuously implemented for state affairs and people's livelihood. His work, *the Book of Lord Shang*, elucidated concrete measures on his reforms.

商鞅强国图

Meng Mu 孟 母

寡母育儿千百难，三迁卓识非一般。
陈情喻物停机杼，堪塑金身立教坛。

三迁教子
［南朝］刘浚

孟氏三迁宅已荒，至今犹说断机堂。
丝成交匹勤方得，身入芝兰久自香。
俎豆容义非贾炫，经纶事业岂寻常。
母贤子圣谁能似？故里千秋尚有光。

  孟母，生卒年不可考，相传姓仉（zhǎng）氏，战国时晋国（今山西省晋中市太谷县东西仉村）人，孟子的母亲。

  孟母克勤克俭，含辛茹苦，坚守志节，在中国历史上受到普遍尊崇。黎民百姓传颂着她的故事，文人学士为其立传作赞，达官显贵、孟氏后裔为其树碑修祠，后人把她与"精忠报国"岳飞的母亲岳母、三国时期徐庶的母亲徐母，列为母亲的典范，号称中国"贤良三母"，而且位居"贤良三母"之首。

Meng Mu was the mother of Mencius. She was a citizen of the State of Jin of the Warring States Period.

Meng Mu was believed to be of superior character and is revered as an exemplary female figure in Chinese history. She was said to have moved her home three times in search of an ideal location for the upbringing of her son. Along with Yue Mu (mother of Yue Fei) and Xu Mu (mother of Xu Shu), she is known as one of the "Three Virtuous Mothers" in Chinese history.

孟母三迁图

Mencius 孟 子

孟子立言求大同，君轻民贵理为公。
先从大处寻真谛，学识巍然一巨峰。

> 君子以仁存心，以礼存心。仁者爱人，有礼者敬人。爱人者人恒爱之，敬人者人恒敬之。
> ——［战国］孟 子

孟子（公元前372年—公元前289年），名轲，字子舆，战国时期邹国（今山东邹城）人，思想家、政治家、教育家，儒家学派的代表人物，与孔子并称"孔孟"，后世尊称为"亚圣"。

孟子主张"性善"，崇尚天道，重视修养。提出仁政（轻刑罚，薄赋税）、民本（民为贵，社稷次之，君为轻）的观点，未被诸侯任用，一生致力于学问和教育。其弟子及再传弟子将孟子的言行记录集成《孟子》一书。南宋朱熹把《孟子》与《论语》《大学》《中庸》合为"四书"，成为明清两代士子们的必读书。

Mencius (372-289 BC), also known by his birth name Meng Ke, was born in the State of Zou (now Zoucheng, Shandong) in the Warring States period. He was one of China's most eminent thinkers, educationists and Confucian philosophers. He was considered to rank with Confucius and was revered as the "second sage".

Mencius asserted the innate goodness of human nature and advocated light taxes and reduced punishment. He was noted for the view that the well-being of people should outweigh that of the ruler. But his doctrine was not adopted by the kings. Mencius's ideas were compiled into the book *Mencius* by his students, and Zhu Xi, a great scholar of the Song dynasty, selected it as one of the Four Books, along with *Analects*, *Great Learning* and *Doctrine of the Mean*. In the Ming and Qing dynasties, the Four Books were the core of the official curriculum for the civil service examinations.

孟子修身图

Zhuang Zi 庄 子

庄生游逸地天间，物我两亡非等闲。
逻辑常由形象释，高山仰止后人攀。

> 天下有道，圣人成焉；天下无道，圣人生也。方今之时，仅免刑焉。福轻乎羽，莫之知载；祸重乎地，莫之知避。
>
> ——［战国］庄 子

庄子（公元前369年—公元前286年），名周，字子休（一说子沐），战国中期宋国蒙（今安徽蒙城）人，哲学家、思想家、文学家，道家学说创始人之一，后人尊称其"庄子"，与老子并称"老庄"。

庄周崇尚自由而不应楚威王之聘，生平只做过宋国地方的漆园吏，几乎一生退隐，无拘无束。庄子研究学问，洞悉易理，深刻指出"《易》以道阴阳"。代表作品《庄子》。庄子善于将抽象的逻辑思维与形象思维相结合，以世间常见的现象来表达深刻的道理，达到世人难以企及的高度，巍巍若泰山，令人仰慕。

Zhuangzi (369—286 BC), with the birth name Zhuangzhou, was born in the State of Song during the Warring States Period. He was an influential philosopher in Chinese history and was regarded as one of the founders of Taoism. He was considered to rank with the great thinker Laozi.

Zhuangzi was an advocate of the carefree lifestyle. He once served as a minor official in Song but spent most of his life in retirement. He was a master of Yili, the classical Chinese studies of changes, and his best-known work was the book *Zhuangzi*, widely revered as a masterpiece of philosophy.

庄周梦蝶图

Qu Yuan 屈 原

本性文人不受拘，天堂地狱任驰驱。
文星灿烂君为首，浊世难容高洁栖。

朝发轫于苍梧兮，夕余至乎县圃。欲少留此灵琐兮，日忽忽其将暮。吾令羲和弭节兮，望崦嵫而勿迫。路漫漫其修远兮，吾将上下而求索。

——［战国］屈 原

屈原（公元前 340 年—公元前 278 年），名平，字原，战国时期楚国丹阳（今湖北宜昌）人，政治家、诗人。

屈原出身于楚宗室贵族，曾任楚国左徒、三闾大夫，兼管内政外交。

屈原品性正直高洁，因政见不合而被流放，著有长篇抒情诗《离骚》，并有《天问》《九歌》《九章》等流传于世，后世称"楚辞"。楚辞标志着中国诗歌由民间集体唱和到个人独创的时代，成为中国历史上第一位爱国诗人，是浪漫主义文学的奠基人。屈原因国破而自沉于汨罗江，1953 年屈原逝世 2230 周年，世界和平理事会通过决议，确定屈原为当年纪念的世界四大文化名人之一。

Qu Yuan (340—278 BC), was a politician and poet of the Warring States period.

Qu was born into the imperial family of the State of Chu. He once served as the Left Minister of Chu and was in charge of state and diplomatic affairs.

Qu was known for his noble and upright character. He was once exiled to the south of the Yangtze River. His best-known works include *Li Sao* (On Encountering Sorrow), *Tian Wen* (Questions to Heaven), etc. His poetry is referred to as Chu Ci poems, meaning verses of Chu.Qu and his poems were considered to have founded China's Romantic literature. When Chu fell, Qu committed suicide by drowning himself in the Miluo River, and was revered as the first patriotic poet in Chinese history. In 1953, the 2230th anniversary of his death, Qu was elected one of the Four Men of World Culture by the World Peace Council.

屈原问天图

Ying Zheng 嬴 政

中原一统立君权，翻过分封历史篇。
莫论秦朝长与短，殊勋异绩已空前。

> 朕统六国，天下归一，筑长城以镇九州龙脉，卫我大秦，护我社稷。朕以始皇之名在此立誓！朕在，当守土开疆，扫平四夷，定我大秦万世之基！朕亡，亦将身化龙魂，佑我华夏永世不衰！此誓，日月为证，天地共鉴，仙魔鬼神共听之！
>
> ——［秦］嬴政

　　嬴政（公元前259年—公元前210年），名政，政治家、战略家、改革家，中国历史上第一个称皇帝的封建王朝君主，世称秦始皇。

　　出生于赵国都城邯郸，13岁继承王位，39岁称帝，在位37年，完成华夏大一统，建立了多民族的中央集权国家。创建了皇帝制度，任命三公九卿（不世袭）管理国家。废除地方分封制，代以郡县制。实行书同文、车同轨，统一度量衡等。并北击匈奴，南征百越，修筑万里长城，修筑灵渠，沟通水系。秦始皇建立的中央集权专制制度，对中国和世界历史影响深远，奠定了中国两千余年政治制度的基本格局。虽然秦代仅短暂十几年，但明代思想家李贽仍誉其为"千古一帝"。

Ying Zheng (259—210 BC) was a famous politician, strategist and reformist in Chinese history. He was referred to as Qin Shi Huang (meaning "the first emperor of Qin") for founding the Qin dynasty, China's first feudal dynasty. Ying was born in the capital of the State of Zhao and became the King of Qin when he was thirteen. He unified all of China and became China's first emperor at 39. He ruled for a total of 37 years.

During his reign, Ying standardized currency, weights, measures, the written language and the length of the axles of carts to facilitate transport on the road system. Besides, he constructed the Great Wall and the Linqu Canal which allowed water transport between north and south China. The central regime of Qin had a profound impact on the later dynasties.

嬴政一统天下图

Li Si 李 斯

理政行文一代强，秦廷业绩正煌煌。
奈何违逆先皇意，转瞬之间家国伤。

> 泰山不让土壤，故能成其大；河海不择细流，故能就其深；王者不却众庶，故能明其德。
> ——［秦］李 斯

　　李斯（公元前284年—公元前208年），字通古。战国末期楚国上蔡（今河南省驻马店市上蔡县芦冈乡李斯楼村）人。秦代著名的政治家、文学家和书法家。

　　李斯从荀子学帝王之术，学成入秦。秦王采纳其计谋，遣谋士持金玉游说关东六国，离间各国君臣，又任其为客卿，不久官为廷尉。秦统一天下后，李斯为丞相，他建议拆除郡县城墙，销毁民间兵器；反对分封制，坚持郡县制。又主张焚烧民间收藏的《诗》《书》等百家语，禁止私学，以加强中央集权统治。李斯政治主张的实施对中国和世界产生了深远的影响，奠定了中国两千多年政治制度的基本格局。

　　秦始皇死后，他与赵高合谋，伪造遗诏，迫令始皇长子扶苏自杀，立少子胡亥为二世皇帝。后为赵高所忌，于秦二世二年（前208年）被腰斩于咸阳闹市，并灭三族。

Li Si (284—208 BC), originally from Shang Cai in the State of Chu (now Shangcai, Henan), was a famous politician, scholar and calligrapher of the Qin dynasty.

Li was a student of the great thinker Xunzi before he moved to the State of Qin. He was trusted by the King of Qin and was sent to sow discord in other six states. After Qin defeated the other six states and united China, Li was appointed the chief counsellor. He made many proposals on strengthening the centralist control of Qin, and was notorious burning many books in public hands to suppress the oppositions of scholars. His thought was considered to have had a profound impact on China's history of politics.

After Qin Shi Huang died, Li and the eunuch Zhao Gao tricked Fusu, the late emperor's choice of successor, into committing suicide and put another prince on the throne. He was later betrayed by Zhao and was executed after being charged with treason.

李斯勤秦图

Meng Tian 蒙 恬

为报军情笔改良，蒙恬夫妇绩非常。
羊毫兔管扬优势，因有兰亭曲水觞。

天要亡我，天之亡我，我何渡
为，天欲亡我，夫复何求。
——［秦］蒙恬

蒙恬（约公元前259年—公元前210年），姬姓，蒙氏，名恬，祖籍齐国（今山东省蒙阴县）人，秦朝著名将领，军事家。

公元前221年，蒙恬被封为将军，攻打齐国，因破齐有功被拜为内史。秦统一六国后，蒙恬率三十万大军北击匈奴，收复河南地（今内蒙古河套南鄂尔多斯市一带），修筑西起陇西、东至辽东的万里长城。秦始皇病死，中车府令赵高同丞相李斯谋划政变，令公子扶苏和蒙氏兄弟自裁。

据传蒙恬与妻为报军情及记事等改进了毛笔制作，因此制笔行业中，蒙恬被供奉为行业祖师爷。毛笔的改进，为后世楷书、行草提供了有利工具，书法随之成为艺术，东晋王羲之《兰亭序》即得于此。

Meng Tian (259—210 BC) was a famous military general of the Qin dynasty. In 221 BC, Meng was appointed as general. He led the troops to attack and conquered the State of Qi. After the Qin dynasty was established, he led a troop of 300,000 soldiers to attack Xiongnu and successfully recovered the region of Henan (now Inner Mongolia). He also helped build the Great Wall. After Qin Shi Huang died, he was forced to commit suicide.

Legend has it that Meng and his wife improved the ink brush in order to record military intelligence. He was thus revered as the founder of the brush making industry. His improvement on brushes was also considered to have benefited the development of Chinese calligraphy.

蒙恬忠信图

Liu Bang 刘 邦

天下英才尽属公，因成两汉五洲雄。
时封时灭情非已，心绪千重付大风。

大风起兮云飞扬。
威加海内兮归故乡。
安得猛士兮守四方！

——［汉］刘 邦

　　刘邦（公元前256年—公元前195年），秦沛郡丰邑中阳里（今江苏徐州丰县）人，政治家、战略家，汉朝开国皇帝，汉民族和汉文化的开拓者。

　　刘邦出身农家，因释放刑徒而亡匿芒砀山，陈胜起义后，刘邦集合子弟响应，攻占沛县等地，称沛公，后被封为汉王，辖巴蜀地及汉中一带。刘邦知人善任，任用张良、萧何、韩信等英才，使汉由弱变强，击败楚霸王项羽，统一天下，开创了两汉几百年基业，汉民族得以雄峙东方。然称帝后，对论功分封的异性王不放心，又逐一灭之。在讨伐英布叛乱后病重不起，作《大风歌》："大风起兮云风扬，威加海内兮归故乡，安得猛士兮守四方！"表达了归乡之显荣同守土之隐忧的复杂心情。

Liu Bang (256—195 BC) was a politician and strategist in Chinese history. He was the founder and the first emperor of the Han dynasty.

Liu was born into a peasant family. He once held a minor position but became a fugitive for releasing prisoners illegally. When Chen Sheng started the uprising to overthrow Qin, Liu followed and captured the region around Pei County. After Qin fell and was divided, Liu governed the Bahu and Hanzhong regions with the title "King of Han". He then appointed several talented advisors, including Zhang Liang, Xiao He and Han Xin, and enhanced the strength of his kingdom. He eventually defeated Xiang Yu and unified China. However, after ascending to throne, he became distrustful of his officials and killed all of them successively. He died of illness after suppressing the Ying Bu rebellion. Liu was also noted for writing *the Song of the Great Wind*, which goes "A great wind came forth, the clouds rose on high. Now that my might rules all within the seas, I have returned to my old village. Where will I find brave men, to guard the four corners of my land?" It was considered a classic in Chinese literature.

刘邦称雄图

Xiang Yu 项 羽

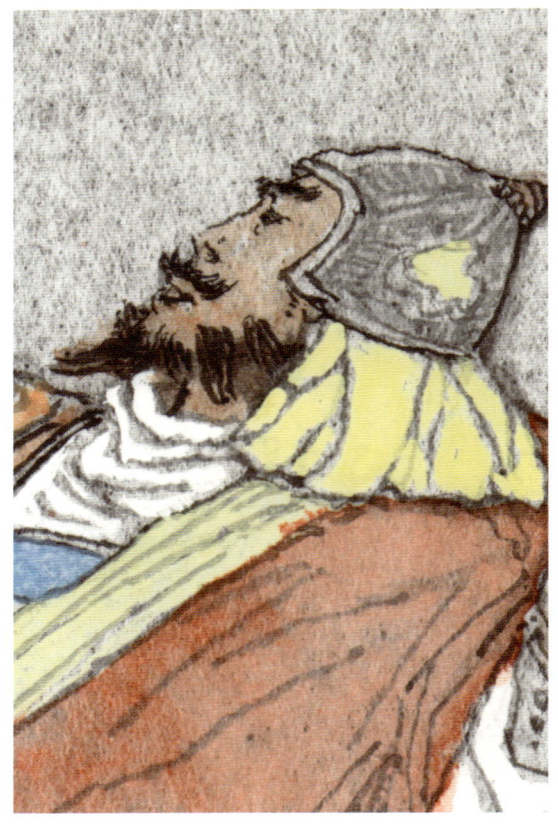

血性男儿思项羽，沉舟破釜众军寒。
秦庭撼动功为首，本纪因能奕世传。

力拔山兮气盖世，
时不利兮骓不逝。
骓不逝兮可奈何，
虞兮虞兮奈若何！

——［楚］项羽

项羽（公元前232年—公元前202年），名籍，字羽，秦下相（今江苏宿迁）人，军事家，中国历史上最著名的勇将之一。

项羽出身楚国名将之后，力能扛鼎，心雄万夫。随同叔父项梁在会稽郡斩杀郡守举兵反秦。巨鹿之战，沉舟破釜，自断后路，领兵打败长期以来气吞如虎、横扫六合的秦军，威震海内。后率军入关中消灭秦军主力，灭秦而分封，称霸诸侯，号"西楚霸王"。项羽推翻秦王朝的功绩无与伦比，而在楚汉战争中败于刘邦，自刎乌江。其英勇气概亦被世代人所称道，当代太史令司马迁将其列为《本纪》记载。

Xiang Yu (232—202 BC), born in Suqian, Jiangsu, was a military leader and strategist. He was considered one of the most prominent generals in Chinese history.

Xiang was the descendant of a general of the State of Chu, and was noted for having great physical strength and high ambitions. He and his uncle Xiang Liang rose in revolt against Qin in Huiji County. He was famous for winning the Battle of Julu, in which he ordered his soldiers to carry only a few supplies and destroy their cauldrons and cooking utensils, and sink the boats they had used to cross the river. In doing so, he made clear to his men that they could not retreat and had no chance of survival unless they defeated the Qin army. He eventually overthrew Qin and proclaimed himself King of Western Chu. However, he was later defeated by Liu Bang and committed suicide at the bank of the Wu Jiang. Xiang was widely praised for his bravery, and the historian Sima Qian wrote a biography of him in the *Records of the Grand Historian.*

西楚霸王图

Zhang Liang 张 良

千金散尽报韩仇，借箸刘邦作运筹。
大事成时知进退，山林道观得悠游。

> 家世相韩，及韩灭，不爱万金之资，为韩报仇强秦，天震动。今以三寸舌为帝者师封万户，位列侯，此布衣之极，于良足矣。愿弃人间事，欲从赤松子游耳。
> ——［汉］张良

张良（约公元前250年—公元前186年），字子房，颍川城父（今河南宝丰）人，汉初政治家、谋略家。

张良先世原为韩国贵族，韩灭于秦后，图谋恢复韩国，散尽家财，结交刺客，狙击秦始皇未遂。秦末率部投奔刘邦，为其重要谋士。在刘邦多次危难之际，出谋化险为夷，长计谋天下，"运筹于帷幄之中，决胜于千里之外"。汉朝建立，辞受封邑三万户，仅请封留地（初见刘邦的小地方），称留侯。功成身退，得以善终。后世称为"谋圣"。

Zhang Liang (250—186 BC), a native of Baofeng, Henan, was a politician and strategist of the early Han dynasty.

Zhang was a descendant of an aristocrat family in the State of Hán. After Hán was annexed by Qin, he spent all his family fortune in attempt to restore the state but could not succeed. He then joined Liu Bang's forces and served as an advisor. His strategies played an important role in building the Han dynasty and was awarded the title of Marquis of Liu after Han was established. He lived his later years in retirement and died in peace. He was revered as the "Strategy Saint".

张良归隐图

Zhuo Wenjun 卓文君

为逐真情月夜奔，抛开富贵入寒门。
当垆卖酒传佳话，知己生成爱侣魂。

> 春华竞芳，五色凌素，琴尚在御，而新声代故！锦水有鸳，汉宫有水，彼物而新，嗟世之人兮，瞀于淫而不悟！朱弦断，明镜缺，朝露晞，芳时歇，白头吟，伤离别，努力加餐勿念妾，锦水汤汤，与君长诀！
>
> ——［汉］卓文君

　　卓文君（公元前175年—公元前121年），原名文后，西汉临邛（今四川邛崃）人，原籍邯郸冶铁家卓氏。汉代才女，中国古代四大才女之一、蜀中四大才女之一。

　　卓文君姿色娇美，精通音律，善弹琴。她与汉代著名文人司马相如的一段爱情佳话至今被人津津乐道。她也留有不少佳作，如《白头吟》，诗中"愿得一心人，白头不相离"堪称经典佳句。卓文君大胆追求爱情，这在封建社会是离经叛道的行为。晚年，司马相如移情别恋的时候，她不像懦弱女人那样逆来顺受，也没有因被伤害而丧失理智成泼妇，而是以诗来警戒丈夫，挽回丈夫的爱情。卓文君的经历为后代的知识女性树立了自由恋爱的榜样。而卓文君夜奔相如的故事，则流行民间，并为后世小说、戏曲所取材。司马相如的文采，卓文君之美艳，被传为千古佳话。

Zhuo Wenjun (175—121 BC), originally named Wenhou, was born into a blacksmith family in Linqiong (now Qionglai, Sichuan) in the Western Han dynasty. She was thought to be one of the "four most talented women" in ancient China.

Zhuo was known for her great beauty and proficiency with music. She was good at playing the *guqin*. The love story about her and Sima Xiangru, the famous scholar of Han, has been very popular in China. Her most-known work was *Bai Tou Yin* (Song of White Hairs), in which a line goes "If her husband is a single-hearted man; Who will not leave her till her hair is white." Zhuo was famous for her brave pursuit of love, which was considered unorthodox in a feudal society. In her later years, when Sima had an affair with another woman, Zhuo handled rationally. She wrote a poem to admonish Sima and managed to recover their relationship. Zhuo was revered as a feminist role model because of her pursuit of free love, and her love story has been a favorite topic in Chinese literature and drama.

文君作诗图

Zhou Yafu 周亚夫

屯兵细柳绝风尘，号令昭明泣鬼神。
刘汉若无周姓忌，皇图未必裂三分。

将在外，军令有所不受。
介胄之士不拜，请陛下允许臣下以军中之礼拜见。

——［汉］周亚夫

周亚夫（公元前199年—公元前143年），沛县（今江苏沛县）人，汉初大将周勃次子，西汉军事家，官至丞相。

周亚夫善于将兵，屯兵细柳，号令严明，皇上来劳军，士兵因无军令不让进兵营。"七国叛乱"时，周亚夫率军平定，三个月消灭叛军。周亚夫忠诚刚直，皇上封异性王，都力谏阻止。后被告有谋反意图，不愿受辱绝食而亡。周亚夫同其父辈一样，都是国家为难时可安定天下之良才。可惜这样的忠臣良将蒙冤，个人不幸，亦是国之不幸。

Zhou Yafu (199 —143BC), was born in Pei County (modern Peixian, Jiangsu), second son of Zhou Bo. He was a general and militarist in early Western Han Dynasty, even became the Premier eventually.

Zhou was accomplished in leading the armies, he stationed in Xiliu, with strict orders. Once the emperor came and consolidated the army, the soldiers stopped the emperor for there were no orders allowing him into the camp. During the "Rebellion of the Seven Kingdoms", Zhou led armies and eliminated the rebellion in three months. Zhou Yafu was loyal and upright, the emperor rewarded him as different surname king, he firmly refused. After being accused has the intention of rebellion, he did not being humiliated, implemented hunger strike and died. As his father and ancestors, Zhou Yafu was the heroes might settle the world when in trouble. Unfortunately, such loyal men was wronged, it was not only personal misfortune, but also the misfortune of the country.

周亚夫忠君绝食图

Zhang Qian 张　骞

关山万里百般辛，交往东西第一人。
佛道文明从此接，丝绸寓意大无垠。

帐夜
[清] 吴兆骞

穹帐连山落月斜，梦回孤客尚天涯。
雁飞白草年年雪，人老黄榆夜夜笳。
驿路几通南国使，风云不断北庭沙。
春衣少妇空相寄，五月边城未著花。

　　张骞（公元前164年—公元前114年），字子文，汉代汉中郡城固（今陕西城固）人，外交家、旅行家、探险家。

　　张骞奉汉武帝之命，两次出使西域，辗转数万里，历尽艰辛。第一次被匈奴抓捕囚禁十年，逃出再西行，历时13年回国。第二次出使西域，历经4年。

　　张骞之行，打通了汉朝通往西域的道路，即"丝绸之路"，沟通了汉与西域之交流，将中原文化传播至西域，又从西域诸国引进了汗血马、葡萄等物种到中原，促进了东西方社会经济的发展。张骞是第一个走出国土考察世界的中国人，其影响和功绩无可估量。

Zhang Qian (164—114 BC), courtesy name Ziwen, born at Chenggong, Hanzhong Prefect (now Chenggu, Shaanxi) in the Western Han Dynasty, diplomatist, traveler and explorer.

Zhang Qian, under the command of Emperor Wudi of the Han Dynasty, made two envoys to the Western Regions, turning tens of thousands of miles and went through hardships. The first time he was captured and imprisoned by the Huns for decade, escaped and returned to China 13 years later. The second time he made a trip to the Western Regions and took four years.

Zhang Qian's trip opened the Han Dynasty's road to the Western Regions, the Silk Road, stimulated the exchange between the Han and the Western Regions, spreaded the culture of the Central Plains to the Western Regions, introduced blood horses, grapes and other species from the Western Regions to the Central Plains, promoted the social and economic development of the East and the West. Zhangqian was the first Chinese who traveled overseas, his influence and achievements were hard to estimate.

张骞出使西域图

Li Guang 李 广

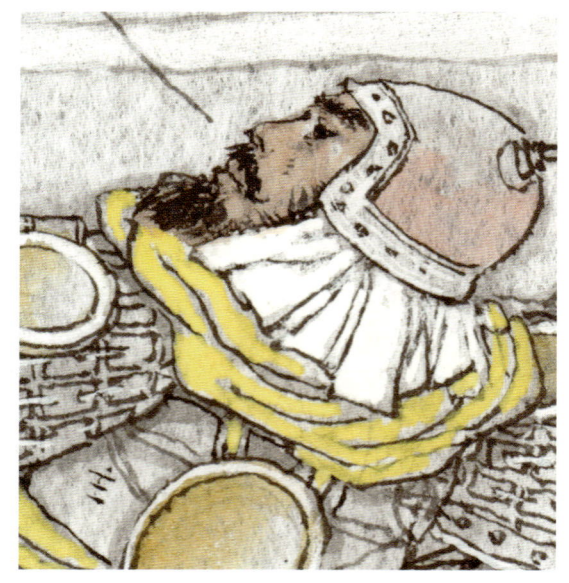

龙城飞将古今钦，盛世疏闲武曲星。
重老崇青皆错失，胸中空有百万兵。

老将行

[唐] 王维

少年十五二十时，步行夺得胡马骑。
射杀山中白额虎，肯数邺下黄须儿。
一身转战三千里，一剑曾当百万师。
卫青不败由天幸，李广无功缘数奇。
自从弃置便衰朽，世事蹉跎成白首。
昔时飞雀无全目，今日垂杨生左肘。
路旁时卖故侯瓜，门前学种先生柳。
苍茫古木连穷巷，寥落寒山对虚牖。
誓令疏勒出飞泉，不似颍川空使酒。
贺兰山下阵如云，羽檄交驰日夕闻。
节使三河募年少，诏书五道出将军。
试拂铁衣如雪色，聊持宝剑动星文。
愿得燕弓射大将，耻令越甲鸣吾君。
莫嫌旧日云中守，犹堪一战取功勋。

李广（公元前？—公元前119年），汉代陇西成纪（今甘肃秦安县）人，军事家。

汉文帝时击匈奴有功任为中郎将，景帝时先后任北部七郡太守，武帝时召为未央宫尉官。曾任骁骑将军，领兵万余出雁门击匈奴，因众寡悬殊被俘，押解途中跃起夺马返回，复任边防太守。匈奴畏怯，称之飞将军，数年不敢来犯。李广不仅作战勇猛，且爱护士卒。李广生于"文景之治"盛世，文景帝重休养生息，尚文轻武；至汉武帝征讨扩疆时，又重用年轻人，李广皆不当时，因有"李广难封"一词。唐代追封古代64位名将，李广在其列。

Li Guang (? – 119 BC), a native of Chengji, Longxi (now Qin'an, Gansu), was a military general of the Western Han dynasty.

During the reign of Emperor Wen, Li was appointed as General of Palace Gentlemen for his achievements in the battles against the nomadic Xiongnu tribes. Later in the reign of Emperor Jing, Li governed seven counties in northern China successively. When he served as commanding general at Yanmen Gate, Li was once captured by Xiongnu in a battle but he managed to escape. Xiongnu nicknamed him "Flying General" and did not launch attacks on Han for years out fear of him. Li was noted for his bravery in battles and his care for the soldiers, but his official career was relatively unsuccessful and he did not acquire the title of Marquis all his life, which was often sympathized with by scholars of later dynasties. In the Tang dynasty, Li was selected as one of the 64 most prominent military generals of previous dynasties.

李广骑射图

Liu Che 刘 彻

刘彻（公元前156年—公元前87年），即汉武帝，西汉第七位皇帝，政治家。

汉武帝雄才大略，开创"察举制"选拔人才，重用人才不论出身、不按级，不问亲疏。在朝廷建立了中朝制，在地方设置刺史。颁行"推恩令"，解决王国势力。将盐铁和铸币权收归中央。思想文化方面"罢黜百家，独尊儒术"。在位54年，国内稳定繁荣。对外开疆拓土，击溃匈奴，东并朝鲜，南诛百越，西愈葱岭，征服大宛，开拓了汉代最大的版图，以"大汉"显于世。并遣使西域，首开丝绸之路，而成中国历史上少有的盛世。然老年猜忌，受巫蛊之祸，冤杀无辜，包括太子，留下遗憾，作"罪己诏"以自责。

Liu Che (156—87 BC) was a politician and the seventh emperor of the Western Han dynasty. He was better known as Emperor Wu of Han.

Liu was noted for his outstanding talents and vision as a politician. During his reign, he adopted many reformist policies to build up the strength of Han: he developed a recommendation system called "Chaju System" to discover and recruit talents, and emphasized people's capability over their background and connections; he also enhanced the central control of the court by appointing "ci shi" (regional inspectors) to keep track of the conduct of local officials; he issued the "Tui En Ling" (order to expand favors) which centralized the power of the imperial court; he created national monopolies for salt and iron and nationalized the issuing of coin currency; he also set Confucianism as the national philosophy. These policies kept the Han dynasty peaceful and prosperous during Liu's 54-year reign.

Liu was also successful in territorial expansion: he led Han to defeat the nomadic Xiongnu tribes, annex the Korean Peninsula, and conquer Baiyue, Congling Mountain, and central Asia. He also sent envoys westward and opened up the Silk Road successfully.

In his later years, Liu became distrustful and killed his crown prince and many of his officials falsely. He at last issued a "zui ji zhao" (imperial edict of self-criticism) to acknowledge and apologize for his mistakes.

一时风虎会云龙，各类英才尽显功。
垂老虽留巫蛊悔，宏图大业总称雄。

秋风辞

[汉] 刘彻

秋风起兮白云飞，
草木黄落兮雁南归。
兰有秀兮菊有芳，
怀佳人兮不能忘。
泛楼舡兮济汾河，
横中流兮扬素波。
萧鼓鸣兮发棹歌，
欢乐极兮哀情多，
少壮几时兮奈老何？

汉武帝盛世图

Su Wu 苏 武

苏武（公元前140年—公元前60年），字子卿，汉族，杜陵（今陕西西安）人。苏武是代郡太守、华夏志士苏建之子。天汉元年（公元前100年）拜中郎将。当时中原地区的汉朝和西北少数民族政权匈奴的关系时好时坏。公元前100年，匈奴政权新单于即位，汉武帝为了表示友好，派遣苏武率领一百多人，带了许多财物出使匈奴。不料就在苏武完成了出使任务，准备返回自己的国家时，匈奴上层发生了内乱，苏武一行受到牵连，被扣留下来，并被要求背叛汉朝，苏武宁死不从。单于将他迁到北海（今贝加尔湖）边牧羊，扬言要公羊生子方可释放他回国。苏武历尽艰辛，留居匈奴十九年持节不屈。至始元六年（公元前81年），方获释回汉。苏武去世后，汉宣帝将其列为麒麟阁十一功臣之一，彰显其节操。

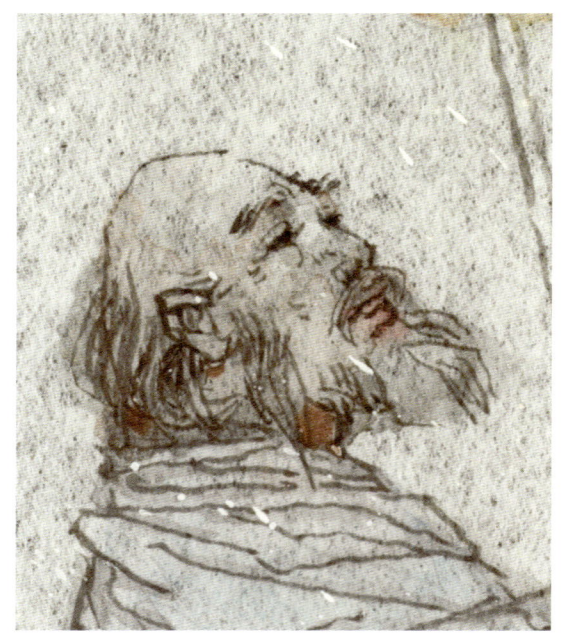

漠北风霜十九年，食毡饮雪伴羊眠。
最难孤寂思乡苦，守节终无愧汉天。

骨肉缘枝叶，结交亦相因。
四海皆兄弟，谁为行路人。
况我连枝树，与子同一身。
昔为鸳与鸯，今为参与辰。
昔者常相近，邈若胡与秦。
惟念当离别，恩情日以新。
鹿鸣思野草，可以喻嘉宾。
我有一樽酒，欲以赠远人。
愿子留斟酌，叙此平生亲。

——［汉］无名氏

Su Wu (140—60 BC) was an official and diplomat of the Han Dynasty. In 100 BC he was sent to Xiongnu, the nomadic tribe in northern China which was rival to Han, as an envoy to show goodwill and express Han's interest in peace. However, Xiongnu detained Su and forced him to surrender and betray Han. He refused and was exiled to Lake Baikal and forced to tend a flock of sheep. Xiongnu announced that he would be released when a ram produced a lamb. Su lived a deprived life in exile for 19 years before he was released and returned to Han in 81 BC. After his passing, in honor of his faithfulness to Han, the Emperor Xuan named him one of the Eleven Outstanding Officials of Qilin Hall.

苏武牧羊图

Sima Qian 司马迁

百代风云笔底来，千秋共仰司马才。
文如判案无欹侧，史苑长存镜鉴台。

> 修身者智之府也，爱施者仁之端也，取予者义之符也，耻辱者勇之决也。以权利合者，权尽而交疏。
>
> ——［汉］司马迁

　　司马迁（公元前145年—公元前90年），字子长，夏阳（今陕西韩城）人，西汉史学家、文学家。

　　司马迁父亲为太史令，受父亲影响，博闻强记，受学于孔安国、董仲舒，后漫游各地，了解风俗，采集传闻。曾任郎中，奉使西南考察。公元前108年任太史令，继承父业，著述历史。坚持以"究天人之际，通古今之变，成一家之言"的志气，创作了中国第一部纪传体通史《史记》，记载了自上古传说的黄帝时期到当世（汉武帝）3000多年的历史。此名篇巨著，文字生动典雅，记事述人不偏不倚，即使对当朝人事亦持公正态度，毫无掩饰，敢于直言，堪为史志样板，被公认为中国史书的典范，为二十五史之首。故司马迁被后世称为"史圣"。

Sima Qian (145—90 BC), born in Xiayang (now Hancheng, Shaanxi), was a historian of the Han dynasty.

Influenced by his father, who served as grand historian at the court, Sima was intelligent and read on a wide range of subjects as a child. In his youth, he studied under great scholars Kong Anguo and Dong Zhongshu and traveled extensively across China. He later entered civil service and conducted an expedition into the southwest of China. In 108 BC, his father died and he was appointed the successor to his father as grand historian, and took over his father's unfinished historical work. Sima was best-known for his groundbreaking masterpiece *Records of the Grand Historian*, which was China's first historical work to record history in a series of biographies. It covered more than 3,000 years from the Yellow Emperor to Emperor Wu of Han. The work was widely regarded as the model of Chinese historiography and Sima was revered as the "Saint of History" by later generations.

子长著史图

Li Ling 李 陵

孤军血战一奇才，太史忠言反受灾。
任是王朝明圣主，终难抵御小人猜。

人之相知，贵在知心。
——［汉］李 陵

李陵（公元前134—公元前74年），字少卿，汉代陇西成纪（今甘肃秦安县）人，军事家，名将李广之孙。

李陵率五千步兵与十几倍于己的匈奴兵战于浚稽山，孤军血战十余日，每日冲锋数十次，最后矢尽人疲，被俘。汉武帝召集廷议时，有人说李陵贪生怕死丧失大节，应灭其族。李陵老母、妻子尽被诛。李陵在《答苏武书》中说自己非偷生怕死、背君亲、捐妻子的人，不死是图有所为以报恩于国主。但李陵最终老死于匈奴，作为悲剧性的人物出现在文人笔下，令人想起唐代王勃"屈贾谊于长沙非无圣主"句。

Li Ling (134—74 BC), born in Chengji, Longxi (now Gansu), was a military general of the Han Dynasty. He was the grandson of the famous general Li Guang.

In a battle against Xiongnu, Li led a troop of 5,000 men and encountered the main forces of Xiongnu, which outnumbered Li by over ten to one. Li and his men fought hard for over ten days but were finally defeated and Li was taken captive. However, Emperor Wu and the imperial court condemned Li as a traitor and had his mother and wife executed. Li Ling lived out his days and died in Xiongnu. He was often seen as a tragic figure by later generations.

少卿思乡图

Wang Zhaojun 王昭君

昭君出塞息烽烟，大汉文传北国边。
何必戏言图画事，和戎本是国之篇。

翩翩之燕，远集西羌，
高山峨峨，河水泱泱。
父兮母兮，进阻且长，
呜呼哀哉！忧心恻伤。

——［汉］王昭君

　　王昭君（公元前52年—公元前8年），名嫱，字昭君，乳名皓月，西汉南郡秭归人，今湖北省宜昌市兴山县人，西汉元帝时和亲宫女。

　　为实现汉朝与匈奴的和睦相处，昭君远嫁匈奴，开创汉匈间长期无战事的和平局面。王昭君的历史功绩，不仅仅是她主动出塞和亲，更主要的是她出塞之后，使汉朝与匈奴和好，边塞的烽烟熄灭了半个世纪，增强了汉族与匈奴族之间的民族团结，是符合汉族和匈奴族人民的利益的，她与她的子孙后代以及姻亲们对胡汉和睦亲善与团结做出了不可磨灭的贡献。

Wang Zhaojun (52—8 BC), originally named Wang Qiang, was a native of Yichang, Hubei.
Wang entered the imperial palace as a lady-in-waiting, and was later sent by Emperor Yuan of the Han dynasty to marry the ruler of the nomadic tribe Xiongnu in order to establish friendly relations. After her marriage, the China's northern borderlands were at peace for half a century. Wang was widely acclaimed for bringing peace between Han and Xiongnu and was considered by many a national heroine.

昭君出塞图

Zhang Heng 张 衡

识君先诵四愁诗，数理原来更出奇，
地动于今难破晓，巨篇灵宪万年碑。

> 且天子有道，守在海外。守位
> 以仁，不恃隘害。苟民志之不谅，
> 何云岩险与襟带？秦负阻于二关，
> 卒开项而受沛。彼偏据而规小，岂
> 如宅中而图大。
>
> ——［汉］张 衡

　　张衡（公元78年—公元139年），字平子，东汉南阳（今河南南阳）人，天文学家、地理学家、文学家。

　　张衡具有多方面的学识才华，文理皆通，善诗文，亦善于制造，尤好天文、阴阳、历算之学。汉安帝公车征拜为郎中，再迁为太史令。在此期间，制造了观察天象的浑天仪，著有天文学《灵宪》、数学《算罔论》等著作。制造了测定地震的地动仪，陇西地震得到验证。张衡文学成就卓越，有《二京赋》《思玄赋》和《归田赋》及《四愁诗》等流传于世。同时对史学、训诂学、绘画艺术、手工制作技术等也精通，堪称全面发展的人物，在世界史上罕见。联合国天文组织将太阳系中的1802号小行星命名为"张衡星"。

Zhang Heng (78—139 AD), born in Nanyang, was an astronomer, geographer and literary scholar of the Han dynasty.

Zhang was an all-round scholar with excellence in both literature and science. He was particularly interested in studying astronomy and mathematics. During his official career, he served in positions including Chief Astronomer and Grand Historian under Emperor An. Zhang developed China's first armillary sphere and invented "Didongyi", the world's earliest seismoscope which forecast an earthquake in Longxi successfully. Zhang was famous for his scientific works *Ling Xian* (The Spiritual Constitution of the Universe) and *Suan Wang Lun* (Discourse on Net Calculation), and literary works *Sixuan Fu* (Rhapsody on Contemplating the Mystery), *Guitian Fu* (Rhapsody on Returning to the Fields), etc. A scholar of rare versatility, he was also a celebrated poet and had good command of history, painting, manufacturing, etc. In 1977 the International Astronomical Union named asteroid 1802 after him.

张衡观天图

Zhang Daoling 张道陵

黄老为宗兴一教，广传天道在人间，
消灾祈福除民疾，世代尊师龙虎山。

张天师草堂
[唐] 常建

灵溪宴清宇，傍倚枯松根。
花药绕方丈，瀑泉飞至门。
四气闭炎热，两崖改明昏。
夜深月暂皎，亭午朝始暾。
信是天人居，幽幽寂无喧。
万壑应鸣磬，诸峰接一魂。
遂登仙子谷，因醉田生樽。
时节开玉书，窅映飞天言。
心化便无影，目精焉累烦。
忽而与霄汉，寥落空南轩。

张道陵（公元 4 年—公元 156 年），字辅汉，原名陵，沛郡丰县（今江苏徐州丰县）人。"天师"为道教门派之一的"正一道"龙虎宗各代传人的称谓。"正一道"（即"天师道"）由张陵（张道陵）创立，后世称张陵为"（祖）天师"。其传人为其子孙世袭，后皆称为"天师"，因此张姓即被称为"张天师"。从元世祖忽必烈开始，官方正式承认"天师"的称号，从此时开始，张天师开始总领江南道教，并在元代中后期，将各种符箓道派都集合在周围，形成正一道。

Zhang Daoling (4—156AD), originally named Zhang Ling, was born in Feng county, Pei (now Xuzhou, Jiangsu). "Heaven Master" is the title used for the successors in each generation of the branch of "Dragon and Tiger" of the "Zhengyi Taoism", a school of Taoism. "Zhengyi Taoism" (namely "Heaven Master Taoism") was established by Zhang Ling, who was called the "Heaven Master" by later generations. The successors were all the offspring of those masters and called as "Heaven Master" in later generations, which was why those with the surname as "Zhang" were called as "Heaven Master Zhang". Since the reign of Kublai Khan, the fifth emperor of the Yuan dynasty, the title of "Heaven Master" was officially recognized by the government. And since then, Zhang became the general leader of the Taoism south of the Yangtze River. He unified various Taoist schools and established the Zhengyi Taoism.

天师降妖图

Cai Lun 蔡 伦

四大文明第一章，诗书赖此传八方。
蔡伦工艺非常事，扬我中华翰墨光。

郴江百咏并序·蔡伦宅
[宋] 阮阅

竹简韦编写六经，不知何用捣枯藤。
自从杵臼深藏后，采楮春桑事已更。

蔡伦（公元60年—公元121年），字敬仲，汉代桂阳郡（今湖南耒阳）人，发明家、造纸术的发明者。

蔡伦任中常侍兼尚方令时，负责管理皇室工场，监造各种器械。在考察作坊时，见缫丝漂絮后，竹簟上留下的一层短毛丝絮，揭下可以用来书写，便收集树皮、废麻、破布、旧渔网等原料，在宫廷作坊施以锉、煮、浸、捣、抄等法，制成植物纤维造纸。这种造纸术的使用，取代了昂贵的丝帛和笨重的竹简，使人类文明传播出现了一次飞跃，是中华民族对世界文明做出的一项重大贡献，大大促进了世界科学文化的传播和交流。蔡伦被封为龙亭侯，奉为造纸鼻祖、"纸神"。造纸术是我国古代"四大发明"之一，蔡伦被编入影响人类历史进程的名人榜。

Cai Lun (60—121 AD), courtesy name Jingzhong, was a native of Guiyang Prefecture (now Leiyang, Hunan) in the Han Dynasty. He is traditionally regarded as the inventor of paper and the papermaking process.

When holding the positions of Regular Palace Attendant and Shang Fang Ling (a eunuch's position), he was in charge of managing imperial workshops and supervising the manufacturing of various instruments. When he paid a visit to workshops, he found that a layer of fiber sheet formed on woven bamboo mat after floating floccrulus of silk reeling process could be used for writing after being stripped down. He initiated the idea of making paper from the bark of trees, remnants of hemp, rags of cloth, and fishing nets by means of filing, boiling, sinking, draining, drying and other processes at imperial workshops. The application of this paper-making method facilitated the replacement of costly silk and heavy bamboo slips, boosted the second-time leapfrogging development of human civilization. As a major contribution made by the Chinese nation to world civilization, it has greatly promoted the spread and exchange of science and culture across the world. He received an aristocratic title Longting Marquis and he was worshipped as the God of Paper-making as well as the Forerunner of Paper-making. Since paper-making is one of the four great ancient inventions in China along with gunpowder, printing and the compass, Cai Lun was also listed in the book The 100: A Ranking of the Most Influential Persons in History.

蔡伦造纸图

Zhang Zhongjing 张仲景

辨证医疗论六经，坐堂问诊播芳馨。
良方永续苍生幸，光耀人间一福星。

> 进则救世，退则救民；
> 不能为良相，亦当为良医。
> ——[汉]张仲景

张仲景（公元150年—公元219年），东汉南阳涅阳（今河南邓州）人，医学家。

张仲景确立了六经辨证的治疗原则，即对各种症候群进行综合分析，归纳其病变部位、寒热趋向、邪正盛衰，而区分为太阳、阳明、少阳、太阴、厥阴、少阴六经病症，基本上概括了脏腑的病变，是中医临床的灵魂。其著述的《伤寒杂病论》是中国医学史上影响最大的著作之一，是学者研习中医必备的经典著作。此书收集、研究了大量方剂，创造了很多剂型。最可贵的是张仲景曾举孝廉，任长沙太守时坐堂问诊，大开衙门为百姓看病，备受尊崇，被后人誉为"医圣"。

Zhang Zhongjing (150—219 AD) was a famous physician from Nieyang, Nanyang (now Dengzhou, Henan), of the Eastern Han Dynasty.

Zhang set up the treatment principle of six channel syndrome differentiation, namely the comprehensive analysis of various syndromes. In so doing, he could conclude the infected part and the condition of coldness and heat, Yin and Yang, thus dividing diseases as six kinds: Tai Yang, Yang Ming, Shao Yang, Tai Yin, Jue Yin and Shao Yin, which basically covered the diseases of organs inside human body and served as the soul of traditional Chinese medicine. He authored the book of *Treatise on Febrile and Miscellaneous Diseases*, one of the classics of the greatest influence in the history of Chinese medicine and the necessary classic for scholars to do traditional Chinese medicine research. This book collected and studied a large number of folk doses and many types of doses had been created. The most valuable point was that Zhang Zhongjing used to be an official in his time through the selection based on filial piety and cleanness. When he acted as the governor of Changsha, he sat in the court and offered medical services to ordinary people, thus had been honored as the "Medical Sage" by later generations.

张仲景造像

Cao Cao 曹 操

不问尔曹奸与忠，经年征战见群雄。
三分天下居霸主，奠定中华一统功。

短歌行
[汉] 曹操

对酒当歌，人生几何！譬如朝露，去日苦多。慨当以慷，忧思难忘。何以解忧？唯有杜康。青青子衿，悠悠我心。但为君故，沉吟至今。呦呦鹿鸣，食野之苹。我有嘉宾，鼓瑟吹笙。明明如月，何时可掇？忧从中来，不可断绝。越陌度阡，枉用相存。契阔谈䜩，心念旧恩。月明星稀，乌鹊南飞。绕树三匝，何枝可依？山不厌高，海不厌深。周公吐哺，天下归心。

曹操（公元155年—公元220年），字孟德，汉末沛国谯（今安徽亳州）人，政治家、军事家、文学家。

曹操出身豪门，少年立志坚韧，能文能武。任丞相后，以汉天子之名征讨四方，内消灭"二袁"、吕布、刘表、韩遂等割据势力，外降服南匈奴、乌桓、鲜卑等，统一了中国北方。并实行一系列政策恢复经济生产和社会秩序，奠定了曹魏立国的基础。在三国中呈强势，为后来司马家族一统天下打下基础。

曹操博览群书，尤喜兵法，有注释《孙子兵法》的《魏武注孙子》传世。诗歌有《短歌行》《苦寒行》等，言辞质朴，情思飞扬，气势豪迈，对建安文学及后世影响很大。

Cao Cao (155—220 AD), also named Cao Mengde, was from today's Bozhou, Anhui. He was a politician, militarist and literary scholar of the Eastern Han Dynasty

Cao Cao was born into an eminent family. He was tenacious since childhood and excelled in both literature and martial arts. After obtaining the position of prime minister, he led his army to suppress revolts in different places in the name of the emperor of Han. He defeated Yuan Shu, Yuan Shao, Lü Bu, Liu Biao, Han Sui and other warlords. He also defeated Xiongnu, Wuhuan, Xianbei, etc. and unified northern China. He implemented many effective policies to restore economic production and stablize the society, laying the foundation for the establishment of the Cao Wei administration. He won many battles during the Three Kingdoms Period and paved the way for the Sima family which eventually unified all of China and ended the chaos.

Cao Cao read on a wide range of topics. He was particularly interested in military strategies and was noted for the work Cao Cao's Commentary on *the Art of War*. He also stood out as a poet. His best-known poems include Duan Ge Xing (Short Song Style) and Ku Han Xing (Song on Enduring the Cold).

曹操征战图

Diao Chan 貂 蝉

羞花闭月艳亦娇，世人只晓沉鱼貌。
其实此身为国生，救民灭贼皆可抛。

原是昭阳宫里人，惊鸿宛转掌中身，
只疑飞过洞庭春。
按彻梁州莲步稳，好花风袅一枝新，
画堂香暖不胜春。

——［明］罗贯中

　　貂蝉（生卒年不详），原名任红昌，传说为山西忻州人，东汉末年美女。
　　当时暴君董卓当道，国难当头，貂蝉为免国家之大灾，随义父王允之意，为国献身，嫁于董卓，意在挑拨董卓与猛将吕布的关系，使连环计，终于借吕布之手除了董卓，红粉英雄流传千古。

DiaoChan, originally named Ren Hongchang, was a native of Yizhou, Shanxi according to legend. She was one of the Four Beauties of ancient China and lived at the end of the Eastern Han Dynasty according to legend.
At that time, the warlord Dong Zhuo had taken control of the imperial court and the whole nation was in difficult times. In order to save the nation from a disaster, DiaoChan sacrificed herself, after being entreated by her patriotic adoptive father Wang Yun, and married Dong Zhuo to turn his godson Lü Bu against him. She eventually succeeded in inducing Lü Bu to kill Dong Zhuo and was revered as a national heroine by later generations.

貂蝉造像

Zhu Geliang 诸葛亮

明知汉祚再难延,六出祁山是枉然。
一诺当年先帝托,满腔热血向中原。

> 天作时不作而人作,是谓逆时;
> 时作天不作而人作,是谓逆天;天
> 作时作而人不作,是谓逆人。
>
> ——[汉]诸葛亮

诸葛亮(公元181年—公元234年),字孔明,汉末徐州琅琊阳都(今山东沂南)人,政治家、军事家、发明家,蜀汉丞相。

诸葛亮青年时耕读于湖北襄阳,有才名,称为卧龙。受刘备三顾茅庐之请,任军师,辅助刘备建立蜀汉政权,赤壁之战大败曹军,形成三足鼎立之势,又夺占荆州,攻取盖州,夺得汉中。公元221年,刘备在成都建立蜀汉政权,诸葛亮被任命为丞相,主持朝政。蜀后主刘禅继位,诸葛亮被封为武乡侯,领盖州牧。诸葛亮鞠躬尽瘁,六出祁山,病死于出征途中五丈原。后世以之作为忠臣与智者的代表。作品有《出师表》《诫子书》等,另发明了木牛流马、诸葛连弩、孔明灯、八阵图等。

Zhuge Liang (181—234 AD), also known as Kongming, was born in Langyadu, Xuzhou (now Yinan, Shandong) at the end of the Eastern Han Dynasty. He was a great politician, military strategist, inventor, and the prime minister of the state of Shu Han during the Three Kingdoms Period.

In his youth, Zhuge worked as a farmer to earn a living and studied in his leisure time in Xiangyang, Hubei. His outstanding intelligence and talents earned him the nickname "Wolong", meaning "crouching dragon". Later, at the invitation of Liu Bei, who desired talents and visited him three times to recruit him, Zhuge became Liu's military advisor. Shu won a historic victory against Cao Cao's troops in the Battle of Red Cliffs under Zhuge's command, which laid the foundation for Shu Han's establishment. In the following years, the Shu army conquered Jingzhou, Gaizhou and the Hanzhong region. In 221 AD, Liu Bei established the state of Shu Han in Chengdu and appointed Zhuge as prime minister. After Liu Bei's death, his son and successor Liu Chan granted Zhuge the title "Marquis of Wu District" and put him in charge of all state affairs. Zhuge was celebrated for his complete dedication to the Shu Han administration. He led the Shu army off Mount Qishan six times to attack the state of Wei, and died in camp during an expedition at 54. Zhuge was revered by later generations as a symbol of unwavering loyalty and exceptional intelligence. His best-known literary works include *Chu Shi Biao* (Memorial for the Northern Expedition) and *Jie Zi Shu* (Admonition to His Son). His famous inventions include the automatic transportation device called the "wooden ox and flowing horse", the repeating crossbow called the "Zhuge Crossbow", and the "Kongming Lantern", which was a type of air balloon for military signaling, etc.

/ 中国古代150位历史名人画传 /
ZHONGGUO GUDAI 150WEI LISHI MINGREN HUAZHUAN

孔明运筹帷幄图

Ban Gu 班 固

熟典通经著述丰，私修国史气更雄。
是非邪正心明了，可惜株连外戚中。

临渊羡鱼不如退而结网。
——[汉] 班 固

班固（公元31年—公元92年），字孟坚，扶风平陵（今陕西咸阳东北）人，东汉著名史学家、文学家。

班固出身于儒学世家，在父辈的熏陶下，班固九岁即能属文，诵诗赋，十六岁入太学，博览群书，儒家经典及历史无不精通。公元54年，班彪去世，班固从京城洛阳迁回老家居住，开始在班彪《史记后传》的基础上撰写《汉书》，前后历时二十余年。后窦宪因擅权被杀，班固受株连，死于狱中，时年六十一岁。

班固一生著述颇丰。《汉书》是继《史记》之后中国古代又一部重要史书，"前四史"之一。班固是"汉赋四大家"之一，《两都赋》开创了京都赋的范例；同时，班固还是经学理论家，他编辑撰成的《白虎通义》，集当时经学之大成，使谶纬神学理论化、法典化。

Ban Gu (31—92 AD), born in Fengling (now Xianyang, Shanxi), was a famous historian, writer and poet of the Eastern Han Dynasty.

Born into a Confucian scholar's family, Ban at the age of nine was already able to compose essays and recite poems. At sixteen, he was admitted to the Imperial Academy (Taixue) in the capital Luoyang, where he read extensively on Confucian classics. When his father Ban Biao died in AD 54, he returned to his hometown, and started the compilation of *Hanshu* (The Book of Han). He worked on the book for more than 20 years. After General Dou Xian lost his political fight and got killed, Ban Gu was arrested as one of his supporters. He died in jail at the age of 61.

Ban was a prolific writer. *The Book of Han* was regarded as another masterpiece after Sima Qian's *Shiji* (Records of the Grand Historian). He was also known as one of the four major authors of *fu* (a major literary form, part prose and part poetry) in the Han era. His *Liang Du Fu* (Fu on the Two Capitals) became a model for others on capital cities. In addition, He compiled a political compendium called *Baihu Tongyi* (Comprehensive Meaning of the White Tiger Hall Discussions), which summarized the discussions on a scholarly conference on the Confucian classics held in the White Tiger Hall.

班固撰史图

投笔从戎屡建功，讨平西域丝路通。
班超不做宫中史，志在边陲万里风。

不入虎穴，焉得虎子。
——［汉］班超

Ban Chao 班 超

班超（公元32年—公元102年），字仲升。扶风平陵（今陕西咸阳东北）人。东汉时期著名军事家、外交家。史学家班彪的幼子，其长兄班固、妹妹班昭也是著名史学家。

班超心存大志，不修细节，但内心孝敬恭谨，审察事理。公元73年，班超随奉车都尉窦固出击匈奴，大获全胜。班超还带领自己为数不多的手下，推翻龟兹国在疏勒国（国都在今新疆喀什市）所立的傀儡政权，重立疏勒故王兄长之子为王，建立新的亲汉政权。公元100年，因年迈请求回国。公元102年8月，抵达洛阳，被拜为射声校尉。同年9月，班超因病去世，享年七十一岁。死后葬于洛阳邙山之上。

Ban Chao (32—102 AD), courtesy name Zhongsheng, a native of Pingling in Fufeng(now northeastern Xianyang, Shaanxi), was a military strategist and diplomat of the Eastern Han Dynasty. Three of his family members — father Ban Biao, elder brother Ban Gu, younger sister Ban Zhao — were well known historians.

Ban Chao cherished high aspiration and defied trivial conventions. With the filial piety from the bottom of the heart, he was also a rational observer. In 73 AD, Ban Chao attacked Xiongnu along with the official Dou Gu and won a complete victory. Ban Chao also led several soldiers to overthrow the puppet regime of Qiuci established in Shule and set up the new political regime. In August 102 AD, He was retired as Protector General of the Western Regions due to age and ill health, and returned to the capital Luoyang. He died there in the 9th month of 102 AD at the age of 71 and he was buried on Mangshan Mountain in Luoyang.

班超赴疆图

Hua Tuo 华 佗

华佗（公元145年—公元208年）字元化，汉末沛国谯县（今安徽亳县）人，东汉末医学家。

少时曾在外游学，行医足迹遍及安徽、河南、山东、江苏等地，钻研医术而不求仕途。他医术全面，尤其擅长外科，精于手术，并精通内、妇、儿、针灸各科。晚年由曹操部下华歆推荐为曹操治病，华佗认为曹操头痛是因中风引起，病根在大脑中不是服汤药就能治好的，需先饮"麻沸汤"（华佗发明的一种麻醉剂），然后砍开大脑，取出"风涎"，才能够去掉病根，多疑的曹操认为华佗要借机杀他，于是命令将华佗收监拷问，致使一代神医屈死狱中，华佗所著的《青囊书》也因而失传。

华佗被后人称为"外科圣手""外科鼻祖"。后人多用"神医华佗"称呼他，又以"华佗再世""元化重生"称誉医术高超的医生。

Hua Tuo (145—208 AD) was a celebrated medical scientist who lived at the end of the Eastern Han Dynasty.

In order to gain more medical skills, when he was young, Hua went on a study tour through the present-day Anhui, Henan, Shandong and Jiangsu provinces. Concentrated on medical science so deeply, Hua did not have any interest about being a bureaucrat, which was the popular choice for the learned man in his day. As a medical scientist, Hua had a comprehensive grasp of medical skills, especially of surgery, internal medicine, gynecology, pediatrics, department of acupuncture and moxibustion.

At his old age, Hua was recommended by Huaxin, a subordinate of Cao Cao the monarch of Wei Kingdom, to treat Cao with stroke. Hua thought that Cao's disease was caused by stroke and was rooted in the brain, so it could not be cured by taking medicine. Hua told Cao that in order to get rid of the disease, he need to drink "Mafeisan" (a narcotic invented by Hua himself), then his brain will be cut for the extraction of the mucus that caused the disease. But the suspicious Caocao thought that it was a crafty plot to kill him, so he threw Hua into jail. The remarkable doctor thus suffered a torture and finally died in prison, and the work *Qing Nang Shu* that Hua wrote was lost as a result. Hua was so influential that after his death, in China the saying "Hua Tuo reincarnate" is used to describe a doctor who own a great medical skill.

时处纷繁战乱中，多灾多难庶民穷。
跋山涉水行乡野，悬壶济世著高风。

> 知人者有验于天，
> 知天者必有验于人。
> ——［汉］华佗

华佗煎药图

Cai Yan 蔡琰

十八胡茄血泪遗，思儿怀土两难离。
多情才女多舛运，铸就人间悲愤诗。

雁南征兮欲寄边声，
雁北归兮为得汉青。
雁飞高兮邈难寻，
空断肠兮思愔愔。
攒眉向月兮抚雅琴，
五拍泠泠兮意弥深。

——［汉］蔡琰

蔡琰（公元178年—？），字文姬，东汉陈留国（今河南杞县）人，文学家、诗人。

蔡琰生于文学大家，父亲蔡邕博学，受家庭影响，从小好学，通文史典籍，擅诗赋，懂音乐。时逢东汉败弱，蔡琰被匈奴掳为左贤王妻，生育儿女。曹操统一北方后，用重金赎回蔡琰，让其将父亲的四千册因战乱而散失的藏书回忆写出，蔡琰背书四百篇。

蔡文姬先经离开故土和亲人之痛，后又承受分别儿女之伤，写下了《胡笳十八拍》《悲愤诗》等名篇传世。

Cai Yan (178—? AD), also named Cai Wenji, born in Chenliu (now Qi County, Henan), was a scholar and poet of the Eastern Han Dynasty

Cai was born into an eminent scholar family. Her father, Cai Yong, was an erudite scholar. Influenced by her family, Cai was an enthusiastic learner since childhood, and read extensively on literature and history. She was good at writing poems and songs, and could appreciate music properly. Later, Cai was taken captive by Xiongnu and forced to marry a Xiongnu prince. She gave birth to two sons during her captivity. After Cao Cao unified the northern China, he paid a heavy ransom to bring Cai back to Han. After her return, Cai recited 400 volumes of her father's collection of ancient books and wrote them on paper at Cao Cao's request.

Cai's most famous works include *Eighteen Songs of a Nomad Flute* and *Poem of Sorrow and Anger*, which reflect the hardship and sorrow of her life.

文姬思乡图

Zhang Zhi 张 芝

龙蛇破壁入云中，跳转翻腾意态丰。
大漠茫茫豪迈气，霓裳广带舞高风。

风软潮生江水平，遥峰隐隐浸寒青。
自从香骨沉波底，独我为诗吊尔灵。

——［汉］张 芝

张芝（？—公元192年），东汉敦煌酒泉（今甘肃酒泉）人，书法家。

张芝出身官宦家庭，少年好学多才，而无意仕途，痴迷书法。"凡家中衣帛，必书而后练（染）之；临池学书，池水尽墨"。张芝将字字独立、笔画分离的章草，改为字字相连、意气承接富于变化的今草，创造了"一笔书"。作品若清涧长源，流而无限，如同其家乡敦煌莫高窟壁画中飞天仙女之飘然，为书坛带来了无与伦比的生机，影响了整个中国书法的发展，因而有草书之祖"草圣"之称，与钟繇、王羲之和王献之并称古代书法四贤。

Zhang Zhi (?—192 AD), born in Jiuquan, Dunhuang (now Jiuquan, Gansu), was a calligrapher of the Eastern Han Dynasty.

Zhang was born into an official family and was hard-working and talented as a child. He had no intention to be a government official, and was dedicated to calligraphy.

He developed the traditional cursive script and invented "jincao" (modern cursive script), which featured writing multiple characters using one continuous stroke. His invention had a profound impact on Chinese calligraphy and Zhang was revered as the "Sage of Cursive Script" and one of the four most talented calligraphers in Chinese history.

张芝发书图

Wei Shuo 卫 铄

下笔行文布阵图，形追万物百般殊。
遒筋力骨成方楷，采得隋侯明月珠。

> 下笔点墨画芰波屈曲，皆须尽一身之力而送之。善笔力者多骨，不善笔力者多肉。多骨微肉者，谓之筋书；多肉微骨者谓之墨猪。
>
> ——［晋］卫铄

卫铄（公元272年—公元349年），字茂漪，河东安邑（今山西夏县北）人，晋代著名书法家。卫铄为汝阴（今安徽阜阳）太守李矩之妻，世称卫夫人。

卫夫人师承钟繇，妙传其法，是"书圣"王羲之的启蒙老师，王羲之少时曾从其学习书法。卫夫人不但在书法艺术实践上有突出成就，不让须眉，而且在书法艺术理论方面也有重大建树。她撰有《笔阵图》一卷，全面深入地剖析了有关书法理论，并提出了自己的看法。主张学习书法要上溯其源，师法古人，反对谙于道理；强调执笔须讲究，不同书体应用不同的执笔法，对书法艺术中的笔、意关系和书家修养等做出了深刻的论述。

Wei Shuo (272—349), born in Anyi, Hedong (now Shanxi), was a famous woman calligrapher of Jin Dynasty. Wei was the wife of Li Ju, the official of Ruyin (now Fuyang, Anhui), and was commonly revered as Lady Wei.
Wei once studied calligraphy under Zhong Yao, and was noted for being the master of Wang Xizhi. She made great achievements in both the practices and theories of calligraphy. Her work *Bizhen Tu* (The Diagram of Strokes) contained a comprehensive analysis of former calligraphic theories as well as her own perceptions. Wei emphasized that the way of holding the ink brush should vary according to the script. Her theories were considered profoundly influential in Chinese calligraphy.

卫夫人习书法图

Wang Xizhi 王羲之

公成书圣或因闲，望族当无生计艰。
散淡功名专注艺，鹅行鹤影意阑珊。

惠风和畅骋怀日，天朗气清俯仰时。
文人天趣清犹水，贤者风期静若兰。
知足一生得自在，静观万类无人为。

——［晋］王羲之

　　王羲之（公元 303 年—公元 361 年），字逸少，东晋书法家。祖籍琅琊（今山东临沂），后迁居会稽（今浙江绍兴）。

　　王羲之出身名门望族与文化大族家庭，从小受到文化熏陶，喜读书，酷爱书法。初拜卫夫人为师，后又转益多师。王羲之散淡功名，一心学艺。曾任将军、刺史、右将军等，崇尚无为而治，专注于临池。王羲之喜欢鹅，欣赏鹅的引颈丰神、从容体态及鹤的闲静高雅、超脱世尘，创作出千古行书《兰亭序》，为历代书家临摹效仿，被誉为"书圣"。

Wang Xizhi (303—361 AD) was a famous calligrapher of the Eastern Jin Dynasty. His ancestral home was in Langya (now Linyi, Shandong), and his family later moved to Kuaiji (now Shaoxing, Zhejiang).

Wang Xizhi was born into an eminent scholar family. He loved reading since childhood and had a passionate interest in calligraphy. He started off as a disciple of Lady Wei and later studied under many other prominent calligraphers. Wang was indifferent to pursuing an official career. He served in multiple official positions, but always devoted most of his effort to practicing calligraphy. He was also known for his fondness for observing the movement of geese. His best-known work was *The Preface of Orchid Pavilion*, which was generally acclaimed as the greatest calligraphic work ever in Chinese history, and he was revered as the "Saint of Calligraphy".

逸少观鹅图

Xie An 谢 安

谢公当日起东山，净扫胡尘指顾间。
为筑新城安社稷，乌衣古巷墨长闲。

> 朝乐朗日子，老啸歌丘林。
> 夕玩望舒，入室鸣琴。五弦清激，
> 南风披襟。醇醪淬虑，微言洗心。
>
> ——［晋］谢 安

谢安（公元320年—公元385年），字安石，号东山，浙江绍兴人（祖籍陈郡阳夏，今河南太康），东晋政治家、军事家，官至宰相。

谢安出身名门，多才多艺，善书法，通音乐，对儒、道、佛、玄学均有较高的素养。性情闲雅温和，处事公允明断，顾全大局，不专权树私。治国以儒、道互补，有儒将风范。其品格和才华历代受人敬仰。

淝水之战后谢安遭妒忌被排挤，退出相位，于扬州步邱修筑"新城"（今邵伯镇），于湖中修筑拦水大坝，有效地防治了水患。

Xie An (320—385 AD), born in Shaoxing, Zhejiang, was a statesman and military strategist of the Eastern Jin Dynasty. He once served as the prime minister in the imperial court of Jin.

Born into an eminent family, Xie was an accomplished calligrapher and musician, and had a good grasp of Confucianism, Taoism, Buddhism and metaphysics. He was a man of gentle character and an upright and just official, and was thus revered by later generations.

Xie was dismissed from the post as prime minister after the Battle of Fei River. He later led the flood control project in Yangzhou and was credited with preventing floods effectively.

谢安儒风图

Tao Yuanming 陶渊明

五斗难为俗吏呼,桃花源里构新图。
田园独爱东篱菊,诗酒江南第一壶。

短歌行
[晋] 陶渊明

结庐在人境,而无车马喧。
问君何能尔,心远地自偏。
采菊东篱下,悠然见南山。
山气日夕佳,飞鸟相与还。
此中有真意,欲辩已忘言。

陶渊明(公元365年—公元427年),字元亮,后改名潜,号五柳先生,东晋浔阳柴桑(今江西九江)人,诗人、辞赋家。

陶渊明出生官宦家庭,曾祖父陶侃乃东晋开国元勋,祖父、父亲任过太守。而陶渊明幼年丧父,在外祖父家长大。外祖父的高士独行风格对其影响很大。渊明任县令时,因不习惯官场虚礼俗习,"不为五斗米折腰"而辞官归里,田园耕读,诗酒自适。《桃花源记》表达了陶渊明自由的理想境界,为世代赞赏。其一生偏爱菊,有"采菊东篱下,悠然见南山"诗句。诗文以清新自然著称于世,开创田园诗派,为中华古典诗歌开辟了新的境界。

Tao Yuanming (365—427 AD), born in Chaisang, Xunyang (now Jiujiang, Jiangxi) was a famous poet of the Eastern Jin Dynasty. He was also known for another name Tao Qian and his literary name "Master Five Willows".

Tao was born into an official family. His great-grandfather was a founding general of the Eastern Jin Dynasty, and his grandfather and father both served as local officials. Tao's father died when Tao was little and he grew up with his grandfather who had a deep impact on him. Tao served as a county's local official for years before he resigned because of disgust at corruption. He was famous for the quote "I refuse to bow like a servant in return for five bushels of grain". He spent the rest of his life farming, writing poems and drinking wine in retirement. Tao was noted for the prose *Taohuayuan Ji* (Peach Blossom Spring), which reflected his desire for a carefree world. Tao was also credited with founding China's Fields and Gardens poetry and enriching classical Chinese literature.

陶潜赏菊图

Xu Xun 许 逊

富贵谁人祈万寿，当知运命属天年。
生民有难君能解，故尔宫祠祭许仙。

许真君铁柱

[唐] 李翔

恐老蛟重作患深，独埋铁柱至如今。
根牢直下蟠江底，势壮长留镇郡心。
神鬼每闻趋夜后，风雷不敢犯塘阴。
无因更走横泉窟，压断祈精气永沉。

许逊（公元 239 年—公元 374 年），字敬之，南昌县（今属江西）人。晋代著名道士，道教净明派祖师，被尊称为许天师。

许逊博通经史，明天文、地理、历律、五行谶纬之书，尤其喜好神仙修炼。公元 280 年，许逊举孝廉，出任旌阳令，治政廉俭，吏民悦服，时人感其德化，立生祠以供其像，后乃弃官东归，遨迹江湖，寻求至道。传说他曾镇蛟斩蛇，为民除害，声闻遐迩，时求为弟子者甚多。

Xu Xun (239—374 AD), born in Nanchang, was a celebrated Taoist priest of the Jin dynasty. He was the founder of the Pure Brightness sect and was revered as the "Heavenly Master Xu".

Xu had a wide knowledge about Confucian classics, history, astronomy, geography, wu xing (the Five Elements theory), and divination. He was particularly interested in the practices for attaining immortality. In 280 AD, he was appointed as magistrate of Jingyang country. He was upright and honest as an official, which earned him a good reputation and people even put up a statue in his honor. He later resigned from office and returned to the east to practice Taoism. Legend goes that he once fought against dragons and killed snakes to rid people of evils, which earned him a widespread fame and many followers.

许逊锁龙图

Xie Lingyun 谢灵运

谢公兴趣在山林，每对奇观每有吟。
天下文才承一斗，不谙时政断清音。

登池上楼
[南北朝] 谢灵运

潜虬媚幽姿，飞鸿响远音。
薄霄愧云浮，栖川怍渊沉。
进德智所拙，退耕力不任。
徇禄反穷海，卧疴对空林。
衾枕昧节候，褰开暂窥临。
倾耳聆波澜，举目眺岖嵚。
初景革绪风，新阳改故阴。
池塘生春草，园柳变鸣禽。
祁祁伤豳歌，萋萋感楚吟。
索居易永久，离群难处心。
持操岂独古，无闷征在今。

谢灵运（公元385年—公元433年），原名公义，字灵运，南北朝时期诗人、文学家、旅行家。祖籍陈郡阳夏（今河南太康），生于会稽始宁（今浙江嵊州）。谢灵运为东晋名将谢玄之孙，世袭为康乐公，因称"谢康乐"。

少即好学，博览群书，工诗善文。历任永嘉太守、秘书监、临川内史等。谢灵运无意仕途，爱访山水，诗作鲜丽清新、境界自然，犹如一幅幅鲜明的图画，开创了中国文学史上的山水诗派，影响了一代诗风。谢灵运虽为文学天才，却不谙时政，后被以"叛逆"罪而害。

Xie Lingyun (385—433 AD), born in Shining, Kuaiji (now Chengzhou, Zhejiang), was an eminent poet, literary scholar, and traveler of the Northern and Southern dynasties. Xie's ancestral home was in Yangxia, Chenjun (now Taikang, Henan) and he was the grandson of Xie Xuan, a famous military general of the Eastern Jin dynasty, from whom he inherited the title "Duke of Kangle" so was also called "Xie Kangle".

Xie studied hard and read extensively as a child, and excelled at writing poems and prose. He served as an official in many positions but his real passion was traveling and admiring landscape. His poems were noted for depicting shanshui (mountains and streams) vividly and he was hailed as the progenitor of the Chinese landscape poetry.

Despite his genius as a poet, Xie's political career was full of disappointments. He was at last charged falsely with treason and sentenced to death.

灵运避政图

Zhu Chongzhi 祖冲之

奇才数学祖冲之，炼古搜今缀术思。
奥妙无传诚可惜，圆周率算世为规。

指要精密，算氏之最者也。
——[唐]李淳风

　　祖冲之（公元429年—公元500年），字文远，南北朝时期杰出的数学家、天文学家、发明家。祖籍河北，为避战乱，其先辈迁江南，后居建康（南京）。

　　祖冲之祖父是朝廷负责建造的官员，因而从小受家庭影响喜欢科学知识，青年时进入科技研究机构华林学省从事学术活动。其主要贡献在数学，所撰《缀术》一书被收入《算经十书》，唐代列入国子监教材，后因太深奥而未得传。祖冲之发现的圆周率，在当时世界上最先进，这一纪录保持了近千年，直到15世纪才由阿拉伯数学家卡西打破。天文历法方面，祖冲之创制了《大明历》，最早将岁差引进历法。机械学方面，设计制造过水碓磨、指南车、千里船、定时器等。另在音律、文学、考据方面也有造诣，还著有小说《述异记》。

Zu Chongzhi (429-500 AD), also named Wenyuan, was a pre-eminent mathematician, astronomer and inventor of the Northern and Southern dynasties. His ancestry was originally from Hebei and later moved to the south of Yangtze River to flee from the chaos of war and settled in Jiankang (now Nanjing).

Influenced by his grandfather, who was an official in charge of construction, Zu developed an interest in science as a child. In his youth, he was admitted to the scientific institute Hualin Xuesheng. Zu was best-known for his contributions in mathematics. His work *Zhui Shu* (Method of Interpolation) became a required maths textbook at the imperial college of the Tang dynasty, but it didn't survive to the present day.

Zu was noted for calculating the approximations of π, which remained the most accurate approximation for almost a thousand years until the 15th century. He invented the Daming calendar, taking suicha (yearly difference) into calculation for the first time. Zu also stood out as an engineer and mechanic. His inventions included the water-powered trip hammer mill, the south-pointing chariot, the paddle-wheel boat, etc. He was also known for compiling the novel *Shu Yiji* (Records Narrating the Strange).

冲之造像

Li Daoyuan 郦道元

百卷奇书万里行，千条水路勘风情。
山川地理人文注，科学文风两大成。

自三峡七百里中，两岸连山，略无阙处。重岩叠嶂，隐天蔽日。自非亭午夜分，不见曦月。

——[南北朝] 郦道元

　　郦道元（公元472年—公元527年），字善长，今河北涿州人，南北朝时期北魏官员，地理学家、文学家。

　　年少时博览群书，幼时曾随父亲到山东访求水道，后又游历秦岭、淮河以北和长城以南的广大地区，考察河道沟渠，搜集有关风土民情、历史故事、神话传说等，积累了丰富的第一手资料。期间还查阅了大量的历史文献，考证了前人的著作400多种，在前人《水经》（15000千字，记述河流137条）的基础上撰《水经注》40卷。全书30万字，记述了1252条河流及有关人文历史。《水经注》句斟字酌，文笔精炼，既是一部内容翔实的地理学著作，又是一部风格优美的山水散文汇集，开我国游记文学的先河。

Li Daoyuan (472—527 AD), also named Shanchang, was born in Zhuozhou, Hebei. He was an official, geographer, and literary scholar of the Northern Wei dynasty.

Li was well-read as a child and once went to Shandong to investigate waterways with his father. He later traveled extensively across China and gained much first-hand materials on China's geography, folk customs, tales, and mythologies, which he incorporated into his best-known work *Shui Jing Zhu* (Commentary on the Water Classic) which contained 40 volumes and 300,000 characters. The work was based on the former work *Shui Jing* (Water Classic) and recorded 1252 watercourses and the history, geography and culture of the surrounding regions at length. It was regarded as the progenitor of the Chinese travel literature.

道元勘察图

Jia Sixie 贾思勰

太守忧劳重本农，民生饱暖在心胸。
躬亲广取田家事，博采前贤一学宗。

贾思勰（公元386年—公元543年），北魏末年益都（今山东寿光）人，曾任高阳太守，农学家。

贾思勰为官期间，到过山东、河北、河南等许多地方考察农业生产，并亲自从事生产劳动，饲养牲畜、栽种粮食等。同时查阅了有关史料，系统地总结了秦汉以来我国黄河流域的农业科学技术知识，著成综合性农书《齐民要术》。全书共10卷，92篇，11万多字，内容包括耕田、谷物、蔬菜、果树、树木、畜产、酿造、调味、调理、外国物产等，是我国现存最早系统、完整地描述农业生产的大型农业百科全书，列为古代五大农书（《氾胜之书》《齐民要术》《陈敷农书》《王祯农书》《农政全书》）之首，也是世界农学史上最早的名著之一，对后世的农业生产有着深远的影响。

贾思勰引谚论种谷树木

齐民要术曰：且天子亲耕，皇后亲蚕。况夫田父而怀窳惰乎。李衡于武陵龙阳泛洲上作宅，以种甘橘千树，吴末甘橘成，岁得绢数千匹。樊重欲作器物，先种梓漆，时人嗤之。然积以岁月，皆得其用。此种植之不可已也。谚曰云云。此之谓也。一年之计，莫如种谷。十年之计，莫如树木。

——［隋］无名氏

Jia Sixie (386—543 AD), born in Yidu (now Shouguang, Shandong) at the end of the Northern Wei Dynasty, was an official and agriculturalist. He once served as the local official of Gaoyang.

When being an official, Jia journeyed through regions including Shandong, Hebei, and Henan to investigate agricultural production. He also engaged in such activities as livestock breeding and crop planting in person. Jia was best-known for his work *Qi Min Yao Shu* (Essential Techniques for the Welfare of the People), which, containing 10 volumes, 92 chapters and more than 110,000 characters, was the most comprehensive encyclopedia on ancient China's agriculture and had a profound impact on later generations.

贾思勰察田图

Li Jing 李 靖

征战沙场气概殊，奇谋勇决若孙吴。
江山赖此虬髯客，四境相邻尽坦途。

> 蛮夷之地，我只需三千轻骑便可。三军将士听令，今次之战，随我深入虏庭，克复定襄，威拭北狄，以振我大唐雄风！
>
> ——［隋］李靖

　　李靖（公元571年—公元649年），字药师，雍州三原（今陕西三原县东北）人。隋末唐初将领，是唐朝文武兼备的著名军事家。后封卫国公，世称李卫公。

　　李靖善于用兵，长于谋略，为唐王朝的建立和发展立下了赫赫战功，南平萧铣、辅公祏，北灭东突厥，西破吐谷浑。去世后谥曰景武，墓葬昭陵。著有数种兵书，惜多亡佚。在李靖的戎马生涯中，他指挥了几次大的战役，取得了重大胜利，这不仅因为他勇敢善战，更因为他有着卓越的军事才能与军事理论。他根据一生的实践经验，写出了许多优秀的军事著作。

Li Jing (571—649 AD), courtesy name Yaoshi, was born in Sanyuan, Yongzhou(northeast of Sanyuan County, Shaanxi Province); general of Late Sui and Early Tang Dynasties, a prevalent military strategist, well established in both pen and the sword; later honored as the Duke of Wei, the Vassal of Li Wei.

Li Jing was expertized in military, accomplished in strategizing, and had elaborated meritorious contributions in the establishment of the Tang Dynasty:conquered XiaoXian and Fu Gong in the south, destroyed Eastern Turks in the north, defeated Tuyuhun heading west. His posthumous title was "Jing Wu", and he was buried in the Tomb of Zhao, accompanying his monarch of Taizong. His monographs were multifarious, but unfortunately the majority of which were lost. In his military life, he commanded several large battles, and achieved great victories, not only because of his bravery, but also for his excellence and military doctrines. He wrote plethora of illustrious military writings on the basis of his practical experience.

李靖用兵图

Wei Zheng 魏 徵

衷心一片十思疏，诸事相谋慎始初。
如若太宗轻镜鉴，凌烟阁上无丈夫。

蛮述怀·出关
[唐] 魏 徵

中原初逐鹿，投笔事戎轩。
纵横计不就，慷慨志犹存。
杖策谒天子，驱马出关门。
请缨系南粤，凭轼下东藩。
郁纡陟高岫，出没望平原。
古木鸣寒鸟，空山啼夜猿。
既伤千里目，还惊九逝魂。
岂不惮艰险，深怀国士恩。
季布无二诺，侯嬴重一言。
人生感意气，功名谁复论。

魏徵（公元580年—公元643年），字玄成，唐代钜鹿（今河北邢台）人，政治家、思想家、史学家，辅佐唐太宗创建了"贞观之治"。

魏徵是中国历史上最负盛名的谏臣，向唐太宗面陈谏议50次，呈送奏疏十余件，谏言达数十万言。其次数之多，言辞之激切，态度之坚定，都为众大臣所难以比拟。著名的《谏太宗十思疏》，从十个方面论述治国之道和修身之理，谏太宗居安思危，谨慎谋事。著有《隋书》序论、《梁书》《陈书》《齐书》总论及祭文诗篇等。死后入凌烟阁，为唐二十四功臣之一，位列第四。

Wei Zheng, (580—643 AD), Xuancheng, was born in Julu (now Xingtai of Hebei); as a politician, thinker and historian, assisted Taizong Emperor who created the "Excellent Governance of Zhenguan Reign".

Wei Zheng was the most prestigious remonstrant in Chinese history, presenting scores of advice to Emperor Taizong, with additional dozens of memorials, cumulative admonitions with millions of characters delivered… The frequency of times, the intensity of his words and the firmness of his attitude were all incomparable to those of other ministers. *The famous Ten Thoughts of Admonishing Taizong*, discussing the principles of ruling the country and cultivating the body from ten aspects, remonstrated Taizong to be prudent and cautious. He published the Preface of the History of the *Sui dynasty*, *The History of the Liang dynasty*, *The History of the Chen dynasty* and the Prologue and Psalms of *The History of the Qi dynasty*. After death, he was worshipped into the Ling Yan'ge Pavilion, as one of the Tang 24 Meritorious, ranked fourth.

魏徵陈谏图

Sun Simiao 孙思邈

中医本有道家风，辨识阴阳转化功。
博采良方寻妙理，凡心圣手世人崇。

取金之精，合石之液。列为夫妇，结为魂魄。一体混沌，两精感激。河车覆载，鼎候无忒。洪炉烈火，烘焰翕赫。烟未及黔，焰不假碧。如畜扶桑，若藏霹雳。姹女气索，婴儿声寂。透出两仪，丽于四极。壁立几多，马驰一驿。宛其死矣，适然从革。恶黜善迁，情回性易。紫色内达，赤芒外射。熠若火生，乍疑血滴。号曰中环，退藏于密。雾散五内，川流百脉。骨变金植，颜驻玉泽。阳德乃敷，阴功□积。南宫度名，北斗落籍。

——［唐］孙思邈

孙思邈（公元581年—公元682年），唐朝京兆华原（今陕西铜川）人，医药学家，被誉为"药王"。

孙思邈自幼聪慧过人，通晓百家，尤崇老庄之学。朝廷征召为国子监博士，拒绝未去，以"济世活人"为终生事业。入深山，访民间，积累药方，著作《千金要方》，是我国最早的临床医学百科全书。晚年应朝廷之请，主持完成了世界上第一部国家药典《唐新本草》。孙思邈医德高尚，是医德的倡导者，后人在道观里供有"药王殿"以纪念。孙思邈还是养生的倡导者和实践者，有一套完整的方法传于世，其年幼多病，然百岁后无疾而终。

Sun Simiao(581—682 AD), was born in Huayuan, Jingzhao (now Tongchuan, Shaanxi) of the Tang dynasty, as a pharmaceutist, was known as the "Master of Medicine".

Sun was intelligent since childhood, proficient in hundreds of doctrines, Taoism in particular. The court conscripted him as the assistant of Directorate of Imperial Academy, he refused. He regarded "serve the living" as a lifelong career. He walked into the mountains, visited the folk, accumulated the prescriptions, formed *the monograph of Thousand Golden Prescriptions*, being China's earliest encyclopedia of Clinical Medicine. At the request of the imperial court, Sun Simiao presided over the completion of the world's first national pharmacopoeia, *Tang New Herbal Medicine*. Sun Simiao appreciated and was the advocator of noble medical ethics, the descendants in the Taoist temple perceiving the Palace of The Medicine Master to commemorate him.

思邈济世图

Li Shiming 李世民

李世民（公元598年—公元649年），生于陕西武功别馆（今陕西省武功县），祖籍陇西成纪（今甘肃天水秦安）人，政治家、军事家，唐代第二位皇帝，称唐太宗。

李世民少年从军，随任晋阳太守的父亲李渊多次出征，后劝父起兵反隋，建立唐朝，封秦王，掌尚书令，统领右军。领兵逐步消灭各地割据势力。登基后，以亡隋为鉴，励精图治。最可称道的是虚心纳谏，鼓励臣下不要顾忌皇上情绪而大胆进言，因此经常忍受指责。政治上，既往不咎，知人善任，整饬吏治；经济上，薄赋尚俭，恢复生产；并致力复兴文教，使隋末动荡之局面得以稳定。对外多次用兵，平定北面、西部及周边势力，令四方宾服。在位23年，史称"贞观之治"，为大唐盛世奠定了基础。

Li Shimin(598—649 AD), was born in the Wugong Annex of Shaanxi (now Wugong, Shaanxi), with fatherland of Chengji, Shaanxi(Qin'an, Tianshui, Gansu), politician, militarist, the second emperor of the Tang dynasty, titled as the Taizong Emperor.

Li Shimin participated in the army in his teenage, and accompanied his father, Li Yuan, who was appointed the Governor of Jinyang, with plethora of expeditions. Subsequently, he suggested his father to set up the army against the Sui dynasty, and establish the Tang dynasty. Hence, he was entitled as the Duke of Qin, took charge of the Chief Imperial Secretary, led the Right Army, whereupon eliminated the separatist forces everywhere. After ascending to the throne, he took the collapse of the Sui Dynasty as a mirror, implemented assiduous governance. The most commendable and praiseworthy of him was the humbly remonstrance, he encouraged officials do not scruple the emperor's emotions and bold advice, thence he endured accusations frequently. Politically, the past was not to blame, to distinguish the good, to rectify the official rule. Economically, to reduce the taxes and to advocate thrifty, restore production, he strived to revive the culture and education, stabilized the turbulent predicaments in the late Sui. Militarily, he made use of foreign troops, pacified the north and the west and peripheral forces. With 23 years' reign, known as the"Excellent Governance of Zhenguan Reign",he laid the foundation for the resplendency of the Tang dynasty.

贞观之治载辉煌，兼听则明暗则伤。
忍耻朝堂承众责，换来社稷百年昌。

春日望海

［唐］李世民

披襟眺沧海，凭轼玩春芳。
积流横地纪，疏派引天潢。
仙气凝三岭，和风扇八荒。
拂潮云布色，穿浪日舒光。
照岸花分彩，迷云雁断行。
怀卑运深广，持满守灵长。
有形非易测，无源讵可量。
洪涛经变野，翠岛屡成桑。
之罘思汉帝，碣石想秦皇。
霓裳非本意，端拱且图王。

世民济世图

Xuan Zang 玄 奘

笃志恒心何此奇，孤行万里极艰危。
虽经九死终无悔，唯识宗开世上疑。

若夫玉毫流照，甘露洒于大千；金镜扬辉，薰风被于有截。故知示现三界，粤称天下之尊；光宅四表，式标域中之大。是以慧日沦影，像化之迹东归；帝猷宏阐，大章之步西极。

——［唐］玄 奘

玄奘（公元602年—公元664年），俗姓陈，唐代洛州缑氏（今河南偃师）人，高僧，法相宗（唯识宗）创始人，佛经翻译家、旅行家。

玄奘13岁始出家游历各地，参访名师。29岁时请允西行求法，未获批准，遂私往天竺。归国后用十几年时间将74部约1330卷经文译成汉语，其中"唯识"（万物唯识）部分属综合创新。理论体系庞大，论证繁多，在世界宗教史上罕见，对中外哲学产生过重大影响。玄奘九死一生舍身求法的精神激励着后人，被誉为"千古一人"。其口授的异国见闻，由弟子整理为《大唐西域记》12卷10多万字，记载了西域见闻，被译为德、法、英、日等各国文字，对世界文化的发展产生了深远影响，玄奘因之成为世界文化名人。

Xuan Zang (602—664 AD), with his surname of Chen, was born in Goushi, Luozhou of the Tang dynasty(now Yanshi of Henan), hierarch, patriarch of Dharmalaksana (Vijnaptimātratā), Buddhist translator, traveler.

Xuanzang commenced travel around the country since the age of 13, visiting prestigious teachers. When he was 29, he asked for permission to travel westward, nevertheless he didn't garner, he went to Tianzhu privately. After returning, he took more than a decade to translate 74 books, approximately 1,330 verses into Chinese, amongst the Volume of Vijnaptimātratā was a comprehensive innovation.

The theory was enormous, the argument was numerous, his verification and illustrations were also rare in the world religious history, having relevance to Chinese and foreign philosophies. Xuanzang's spirit of sacrificing his life to seek the Dharma inspired his descendants to name him as "*a man of a thousand ages*". His oral foreign experience, compiled by his disciples into The Book of the Western Regions of the Tang dynasty in 12 volumes with more than 100,000 words, recorded the Western Regions, was translated into German, French, English, Japanese and other languages, having a profound impact on the development of world culture. Xuanzang has become the world prestigious people.

玄奘取经图

Empress Zhangsun 长孙皇后

献谋雅韵助夫君,简略家风约族群。
有识良臣无后顾,雍容懿德史铭文。

春游曲
[唐] 长孙皇后

上苑桃花朝日明,兰闱艳妾动春情。
井上新桃偷面色,檐边嫩柳学身轻。
花中来去看舞蝶,树上长短听啼莺。
林下何须远借问,出众风流旧有名。

    文德皇后长孙氏(公元601年—公元636年),小字观音婢,河南洛阳人,唐朝宰相长孙无忌同母妹,唐太宗(李世民)的皇后。

    长孙氏13岁嫁李世民,武德末年,她竭力争取李渊后宫对李世民的支持,玄武门之变当天,她亲自勉慰诸将士,之后拜太子妃,李世民即位后册封其为皇后。她善于借古喻今,指出李世民为政的失误,并保护忠诚、正直、得力的大臣。长孙皇后利用自身对皇帝的影响力来护慰朝廷贤良,匡正丈夫的过失。一方面欣赏并庇护魏徵那些敢于直言的忠臣,另一方面也不时提醒李世民要行仁政。她以女性特有的力量在男权至上的封建社会发挥独特的作用辅佐皇帝,使得初唐出现了非常和谐的政治局面。

Empress Zhangsun (601—636 AD), with little style name of Guanyin Maidservant, was born in Luoyang, Henan, younger sister of Zhangsun Wuji, (the Premier of the Tang Dynasty), Emperor Taizong's queen.

Zhangsun married Li Shimin when she was 13, by the late Wude reign, she tried her best to win Li Yuan's concubines' support. On the Event of Xuanwu Gate, she personally consoled the generals, and then rewarded as the princess. After Li Shimin ascended the throne, she was crowned queen. She was good at imitating the past, pointing out the mistakes of Li Shimin's administration and protecting the ministers of integrity. Zhangsun used her influence on the emperor to protect the court's virtuous and correct her husband's mistakes. On the one hand, she appreciated and protected those loyal officials dared to speak out. On the other hand, Li Shimin was reminded from time to time to practice benevolence. She played a unique role in the patriarchal feudal society with the unique power of women to assist the emperor, making the early Tang dynasty in a relatively harmonious political situation.

长孙皇后造像

Wu Zetian 武则天

贞观续继启开元，一代鸿猷效轩辕。
帝国从来男作主，乾陵碑上复何言。

唐享昊天乐·五

[唐] 武则天

朝坛雾卷，曙岭烟沉。
爰设筐币，式表诚心。
筵辉丽璧，乐畅和音。
仰惟灵鉴，俯察翘襟。

    武则天（公元 624 年—公元 705 年），祖籍并州文水县（现山西文水县东），生于长安（今陕西省西安市），中国历史上唯一得到普遍承认和众人皆知的女皇帝。

    十四岁入后宫为唐太宗的才人，唐太宗赐号"武媚"，唐高宗时初为昭仪，后为皇后（公元 655 年—公元 683 年），尊号为天后，与唐高宗李治并称二圣。公元 683 年—公元 690 年作为唐中宗、唐睿宗的皇太后临朝称制，是中国历史上唯一一位女性太上皇。后自立为武周皇帝，宣布改唐为周，定洛阳为都。在位前后，她"明察善断"，多权略，善用人，使得贤才辈出。神龙元年农历十一月廿六日，武氏在上阳宫病死，时年 82 岁。后与高宗合葬乾陵，留下一座无字碑供后人猜疑千年。

Wu Zetian (624—705 AD), also named Wu Zhao, her ancestral place being Wenshui, Bingzhou (now east Wenshui, Shanxi), was born in Chang'an (now Xi'an), solely ubiquitous acknowledged and prestigious Empress in Chinese history.

At the age of 14, she was selected into the harem of Emperor of Taizong, and was given a nickname "Wumei". During the reign of Gaozong (655—683 AD), she was titled as concubine "Zhaoyi", and subsequently the Queen, being worshiped as the "bisaints" with the Emperor Gaozong, Li Zhi. In 683 and 690, she took the throne as the Empress Dowager of the Emperors of Zhongzong and Ruizong, was the sole female overlord. Thence, she crowned herself as Emperor of Wu Zhou dynasty, altered the title of the dynasty from Tang to Zhou, and made Luoyang as the capital. After she took the throne, she was scrutinized and strategic, enabling talents to come across. On lunar calendar Nov. 26th, 705 AD, Wu Zetian passed away at Shangyang Palace, at the age of 82. She was buried with the Emperor Gaozong in the Tomb of Qian, and left with a nameless monument for offspring's suspicions.

武皇上朝图

Di Renjie 狄仁杰

有史传名断案神，明查细察究原真。
冤情能雪民心定，正义通行政界春。

奉和圣制夏日游石淙山
[唐] 狄仁杰

宸晖降望金舆转，仙路峥嵘碧涧幽。
羽仗遥临鸾鹤驾，帷宫直坐凤麟洲。
飞泉洒液恒疑雨，密树含凉镇似秋。
老臣预陪悬圃宴，馀年方共赤松游。

　　狄仁杰（公元630年—公元700年），字怀英，并州太原（今山西太原）人，唐代武周时期政治家。

　　狄仁杰出身于太原狄氏，早年以明经及第，历任大理寺丞、侍御史、宁州刺史、洛州司马等职，以不畏权贵著称。公元691年9月，狄仁杰升任宰相，担任地官侍郎、同平章事，但在相位仅四个月便被酷吏来俊臣诬陷谋反，夺职下狱，平反后贬为彭泽县令。他在营州之乱时被起复，并于公元697年再次拜相，担任鸾台侍郎、同平章事，进拜纳言。公元700年，狄仁杰进拜内史，于同年九月病逝，追赠文昌右相，谥号文惠。唐朝复辟后，追赠司空、梁国公。当时，前任刺史为了抵御契丹，尽召百姓入城，缮修守城器具。但狄仁杰到任后，却让百姓返田耕作。魏州百姓争相立碑颂德。

Di Renjie (630—700 AD), courtesy name Huaiying, was born in Taiyuan, Bingzhou(now Taiyuan, Shanxi), prestigious politician in Tang and Wuzhou Dynasties.

Di originated from Di's in Taiyuan, garnered Mingjing Degree in his teenage, served as Executive of Dali Temple, assistant of Imperial Censor, Governor of Ningzhou, General of Luozhou, and was known for defying the elites. In September, 691, Di Renjie was promoted to the rank of prime minister, serving as a magistrate's servant and a minister of the same pingzhang. In conjunction with the Central Ministry and the Menxia Ministry, he scrutinized the documents and affairs. Nevertheless, in the phase with only four months, Di was falsely accused of rebellion by the cruel official of Lai Junchen, seized and put into prison. After rehabilitation, he was demoted as the Magistrate of PengZe County. He was revived during the Yingzhou Rebellion and appointed as Premier again in 697 and upgraded in 700. He passed away on Sept. 700 he was. additionally titled with Right Premier of Wenchang and posthumous title Wenhui.

仁杰断案图

Hui Neng 慧 能

求法慧能经苦劳，持家南岭赖柴刀。
身贫愈坚心中志，识出磨难见性高。

菩提本无树，明镜亦非台，
本来无一物，何处惹尘埃。

——［唐］慧能

慧能（公元 638 年—公元 713 年），被尊为"禅宗六祖"，对中国佛教以及禅宗的弘化具有深刻和现实的意义。

慧能得到五祖弘忍传授衣钵，继承了东山法脉并建立了南宗，弘扬"直指人心，见性成佛"的顿教法门。他弘化于岭南，对周边地区以及海外文化也具有一定的影响，同时也得到了中原皇室的尊重和供养，皇室屡次迎请慧能进宫，并为其建寺造塔。在滑台大云寺的无遮大会之后，通过对南北是非的辩论，奠定了曹溪禅在禅宗的地位。 武宗灭法之后，曹溪禅即位居中国佛教的主流地位。

Hui Neng (638—713 AD), being respected as "the Sixth Ancestor of Zen" had profound and realistic significance for Chinese Buddhism and the popularization of Zen.

Hui Neng received the Fifth Ancestor , preached the mantle, inherited the Dongshan Dharma and set up the Nanzong, carried forward the "Whether a person can become a Buddha depends on his comprehension of human suffering in his heart. As long as he knows, he can become a Buddha." Dhamma. He promoted indoctrination in Lingnan having, a certain influence on the border region and overseas culture . He also appreciated royal family's respect and support of the Central Plains, the royal families repeatedly invited Hui Neng into the palace, built pagodas and temples. After the Opening Meeting held in the Great Cloud Temple at Hua Tai, in terms of the debate of the Verification between north and south, he consolidated the status of Caoxi School in Zen. After the Wuzong Emperor's Buddhism extinction,, Caoxi Zenism took predominant predicament in Chinese Buddhism.

六祖参禅图

Princess Wencheng 文成公主

盛唐公主吐蕃行,带去中原万里情。
汉藏交和无战事,言功最是播文明。

陇西行四首·其二

[唐] 陈陶

誓扫匈奴不顾身,
五千貂锦丧胡尘。
可怜无定河边骨,
犹是春闺梦里人!

　　文成公主(公元625年—公元680年),祖籍山东济宁(今任城),汉名无记载。

　　公元634年,吐蕃赞普松赞干布遣使大唐,唐太宗遣行人冯德遐出使吐蕃。松赞干布再次派人到唐朝,提出要娶一位唐朝公主,遭到唐太宗的拒绝。公元638年,松赞干布出兵,直逼唐朝松州(今四川松潘),扬言若不和亲,便率兵大举入侵唐朝。牛进达率领唐军先锋部队击败了吐蕃军,松赞干布大惧,在唐军主力到达前再次请婚,派部下薛禄东赞携黄金五千两及相等数量的其他珍宝正式下聘礼。唐太宗将一宗室女封为公主,即文成公主,嫁给松赞干布,成为汉藏民族永远友好下去的纽带。

Princess Wencheng (625—680 AD), with ancestral place of Jining, Shandong (now Rencheng), had her Chinese name lost without records.

In 634, the Btsan Po of Tibet, Songtsen Gampo sent envoys to Tang, Taizong appointed Feng Dexia to Tibet. Subsequently, Songtsen dispatched ambassadors again and requested a princess for marriage, but refused by Taizong. In 638, Songtsen launched a battle to Songzhou (now Songpan, Sichuan). He threatened to invade Tang if he Tang did not marry a princess to him. Niu Jinda led the vanguard forces defeated Tibetans, Songtsen was astonished. He requested for marriage again before the main force of Tang arrived, appointed ga tong zain yü sun with 5000 Liang of gold and equivalent treasures to Chang'an as formal dowry. Emperor Taizong conferred a clan princess, Princess Wencheng, to be married to Songtsen. The marriage became the eternal ties between Chinese and Tibetans.

公主进藏图

Shangguan Wan'er 上官婉儿

上官婉儿（公元664年—公元710年），复姓上官，小字婉儿，又称上官昭容，陕州陕县（今河南省三门峡市陕县）人，祖籍陇西上，唐代女官、诗人、皇妃。

唐中宗时，封为昭容，权势更大，在政坛、文坛有着显要地位，从此以皇妃的身份掌管内廷与外朝的政令文告。曾建议扩大书馆，增设学士，在此期间主持风雅，代朝廷品评天下诗文，一时词臣多集其门，《全唐诗》收其诗三十二首。公元710年，临淄王李隆基起兵发动唐隆政变，与韦后同时被杀。

上官婉儿以一介女流，影响一代文风，这在中国古代文学史上是很少见的。她不仅以其诗歌创作实绩，而且通过选用人才、品评诗文等文学活动倡导并转移了一代文风，成为中宗文坛的标志者和引领者。对于当时文坛的繁荣和诗歌艺术水平的提升具有重要作用。

巾帼庙堂三十年，从容策对日成篇。
书藏万卷兴文馆，山水盛唐诗领先。

彩书怨

[唐] 上官婉儿

叶下洞庭初，思君万里馀。
露浓香被冷，月落锦屏虚。
欲奏江南曲，贪封蓟北书。
书中无别意，惟怅久离居。

Shangguan Wan'er (664—710 AD), with surname Shangguan, little style name Wan'er, also called Shangguan Zhaorong, was born in Shanxian, Shanzhou (now Shan County, Sanmenxia, Henan), with ancestral place of LongXi, female court official of the Tang dynasty, poet, concubine.

During the reign of Zhongzong Emperor, she was conferred as Zhaorong, garnered much sovereign power, perceived prestigious status in politics and literary arena; with the status of imperial concubine, she took in charge of the chamberlain and the outside decree proclamation. She proposed the expansion of library, the addition of bachelors; during this period of elegance, she judged the poems and articles on behalf of the court, plethora of officials set her door, All Tang Poems received her 32 poems. In 710, Li Longji, the Duke of Linzi at that time, launched the Tanglong Mutiny, Shangguan was killed with Queen Wei contemporaneously.

Shangguan Wan'er, as a female, had her influence on the literary style of a generation, which was rare in the history of ancient Chinese literature. She was not only reputed with her poetry creation, selection of talents, evaluation of poetry and other literary activities to promote and transfer a generation of style, but also became the symbol and guidance of the literary world. She was relevant in the prosperity of the literary world and the improvement of the artistic level of poetry at that time.

昭容驭政图

Wu Daozi 吴道子

新意原于法度中,别开蹊径取天工。
消停画笔师张旭,壮阔初唐豪迈风。

王维吴道子画
[宋]苏轼

何处访吴画,普门与开元。
开元有东塔,摩诘留手痕。
吾观画品中,莫如二子尊。
道子实雄放,浩如海波翻。
当其下手风雨快,笔所未到气已吞。
亭亭双林间,彩晕扶桑暾。
中有至人谈寂灭,悟者悲涕迷者手自扪。
蛮君鬼伯千万万,相排竞进头如鼋。
摩诘本诗老,佩芷袭芳荪。
今观此壁画,亦若其诗清且敦。
祇园弟子尽鹤骨,心如死灰不复温。
门前两丛竹,雪节贯霜根。
交柯乱叶动无数,一一皆可寻其源。
吴生虽妙绝,犹以画工论。
摩诘得之于象外,有如仙翮谢笼樊。
吾观二子皆神俊,又于维也敛衽无间言。

吴道子(公元 680 年—公元 758 年),又名道玄,唐代阳翟(今河南禹县)人,画家,中国山水画之祖师,被称为"画圣"。

吴道子少时孤贫,年轻时即有画名。曾任兖州瑕丘(今山东滋阳)县尉,不久即辞职。后流落洛阳,从事壁画创作。开元年间以善画被召入宫廷,历任供奉、内教博士。曾随书法家张旭,感染创新精神;观赏公孙大娘舞剑,体会用笔之道。擅佛道,工于神鬼、人物、山水、鸟兽、草木、楼阁等题材的创作,尤精于佛道、人物,长于壁画创作,"吴带当风"典出于其人物画。

Wu Daozi (680—758 AD), also named Daoxuan,, was born in Yangdi(now Yu County in Henan), artist, the ancestor of Chinese landscape painting, known as "Painting Saint."

Wu Daozi was lonely and poor when he was young. He was appointed as a county lieutenant of Xiaqiu, Yanzhou (now Ziyang, Shandong) and soon resigned. After living in Luoyang, he was engaged in mural creation. During the Kaiyuan reign, he was summoned to the palace with good painting, and served for the officials. He had followed Zhang Xu, a calligrapher, was inspired by the spirit of innovation. And watched Dame Sun playing the sword, and experienced the way of using pens. He appreciated Buddhism well, working on the creation of deities, figures, mountains and rivers, birds and beasts, plants and trees, pavilions and other subjects, Buddhist and Taoism, figures and mural creation in particular. "Excellent drawing skills and elegant style" originates from his portraits drawings.

中国古代 150 位历史名人画传

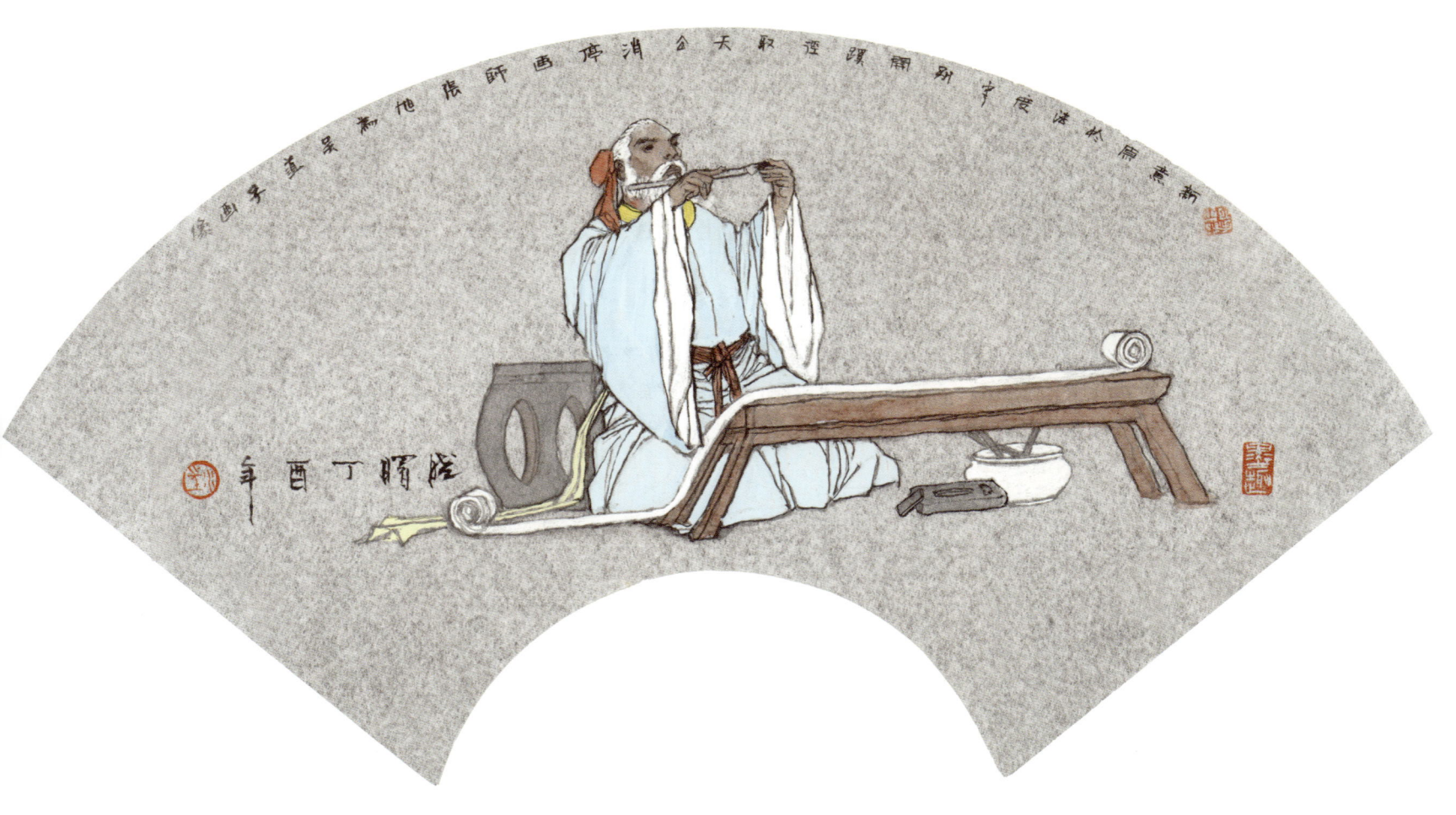

道子作画图

Jian Zhen 鉴 真

传法扶桑为友邻，风惊浪险万千辛。
律宗文父标盛誉，漆像回乡独鉴真。

> 为是法事也，何惜生命？
> 诸人不去，我即去耳。
>
> ——[唐]鉴 真

　　鉴真（公元688年—公元763年），唐朝僧人，俗姓淳于，广陵江阳（今江苏扬州）人；律宗南山宗传人，也是日本佛教南山律宗的开山祖师，著名医学家。

　　曾担任扬州大明寺主持，应日本留学僧请求，先后六次东渡，弘传佛法，促进了文化的传播与交流。公元763年6月25日，鉴真在唐招提寺圆寂，终年76岁。日本人民称鉴真为"天平之甍"，意为他的成就足以代表天平时代文化的屋脊（比喻高峰、最高成就）。

　　在佛教建筑、雕塑等方面，他也颇多建树。在医药学方面，博达多能，品鉴极精，曾主持过大云寺的悲田院，为人治病，亲自为病者煎调药物，医道甚高。

Jian Zhen (688—763 AD), monk of Tang Dynasty, surname Chunyu, born in Guangling, Jiangyang(now Yangzhou, Jiangsu), inheritance of Nanshan Viyana and the patriarch of Japanese Buddhism Nanshan Viyana, prestigious medical scientist.

He once presided over the Daming Temple in Yangzhou and passed six times to Japan at the request of Japanese monks studying abroad, spreading Buddhism and promoting the dissemination and exchange of culture. On June 25, 763, Jianzhen passed away in Toshodai Temple at the age of 76. The Japanese called Jianzhen's death "TianPing Death", indicating his achievements were the roof of the culture of the Tianping era (metaphors of peak and summit).

鉴真东渡图

Li Bai 李 白

太白一生诗酒友，蹉跎屈就谪仙人。
长安不敬疏狂客，满腹文章落世尘。

为宣州谢朓楼饯别校书叔云
［唐］李白

弃我去者，昨日之日不可留；
乱我心者，今日之日多烦忧。
长风万里送秋雁，对此可以酣高楼。
蓬莱文章建安骨，中间小谢又清发。
俱怀逸兴壮思飞，欲上青天览明月。
抽刀断水水更流，举杯销愁愁更愁。
人生在世不称意，明朝散发弄扁舟。

李白（公元701年—公元762年），字太白，号青莲居士，又号"谪仙人"，唐代陇西成纪（今甘肃秦安）人，生于四川江油，一说生于碎叶城（今吉尔吉斯斯坦）。是唐代伟大的浪漫主义诗人，被后人誉为"诗仙"，与杜甫并称为"李杜"。

唐玄宗欣赏其才华，供奉翰林，作文学随从。然因藐视权贵，批评社会，被"赐金放还"，离开长安。李白爱好自然，喜游名山大川，性格爽朗大方，喜饮酒、作诗、结交，其诗中酒多友多，充满真挚的情感，表现出积极的人生态度。李白的诗被世人争相传诵，得以保留近千首。

Li Bai (701—762 AD), courtesy name Taibai, literary name Qinglian Jushi, was born in Jiangyou, Sichuan or Suyab (now Kyrgyzstan). His ancestral home was in Chengji, Longxi (now Qin'an, Gansu). Li was a prominent romantic poet of the Tang dynasty. He was revered as "Shi Xian" (meaning "Poet Transcendent" or "Immortal Poet") by later generations. Li and Du Fu are generally thought to be the two greatest poets in Chinese history and are often referred to as "Lidu" together.

With his talents appreciated by Emperor Xuanzong of Tang, Li once held a post as imperial scholar at the Hanlin Academy. But he was later dismissed and sent away from the capital Chang'an for offending powerful officials at the court and criticizing the society. Li had a frank and generous personality and his poetry reflected his intense love of nature and traveling, the joys of drinking wine, the pleasures of friendship, and his positive attitude to life. Li's poetry retains an enduring popularity in Chinese history and around a thousand of his poems are extant today.

太白吟诗图

Wang Wei 王　维

诗情画意古今雄，山水清新笔力工。
盛世开元添彩色，儒生悟得道禅通。

渭城曲·送元二使安西
[唐] 王维

渭城朝雨浥轻尘，客舍青青柳色新。
劝君更尽一杯酒，西出阳关无故人。

　　王维（公元 701 年—公元 761 年，一说公元 699 年—公元 761 年），唐朝河东蒲州（今山西运城）人，祖籍山西祁县，唐朝著名诗人、画家。

　　公元 731 年，王维状元及第，历官右拾遗、监察御史、河西节度使判官。唐玄宗天宝年间，王维拜吏部郎中、给事中。唐肃宗乾元年间任尚书右丞，故世称"王右丞"。王维参禅悟理，学庄信道，精通诗、书、画、音乐等，以诗盛名于开元、天宝年间，尤长五言，多咏山水田园，与孟浩然合称"王孟"，有"诗佛"之称。书画特臻其妙，后人推其为南宗山水画之祖。存诗 400 余首，代表诗作有《相思》《山居秋暝》等。著作有《王右丞集》《画学秘诀》。

Wang Wei (701—761 AD, 699—761 AD), born in Puzhou, Hedong of the Tang Dynasty (now Yuncheng, Shanxi), with ancestral place of Qi County of Shanxi, prestigious poet of the Tang Dynasty, painter.

In 731, Wang Wei was the First in the Imperial Examination, then occupied in Right Pickup, Investigating Censor, Hexi Governor assistant. During the Tianbao Reign of the Xuanzong Emperor, Wangwei became the Assistant of the emperor and Right Premier during the Qianyuan reign of Suzong Emperor, so he was called the "Right Premier Wang". Wangwei appreciated Zen and Taoism, was proficient in poetry, books, paintings, music, etc. His poems were prosperous during Kaiyuan and Tianbao reigns, five characters per line in particular, depicting the odes of natural sceneries. He is known as "poet of Buddhist". His calligraphies and paintings were marvelous, and he was regarded as the ancestor of South Chinese landscape paintings. His poems were left for about 400 *Lovesickness*, *Autumn Evening in the Mountains* etc. There are also collections of his works, for instance, *Collections of the Right Premier Wang*, *The Secret of Painting and Calligraphy*.

/ 中国古代150位历史名人画传 /
ZHONGGUO GUDAI 150WEI LISHI MINGREN HUAZHUAN

王维向佛图

Yan Zhenqin 颜真卿

颜真卿（公元709年—公元784年），字清臣，别号应方，唐代京兆万年（今陕西西安）人，祖籍琅玡（今山东费县）。政治家、书法家。

"安史之乱"时，颜真卿联络从兄颜杲卿（常山）率义军对抗叛军，颜氏一门30多人殉难，忠心可鉴。后官至吏部尚书、太子师，封鲁郡公，人称颜鲁公。颜真卿立朝正色、刚而有礼，不阿权贵不媚上，以义烈名于时。公元784年，遭宰相卢杞陷害，被派遣晓谕叛将李希烈，凛然拒贼，终被缢杀。

颜真卿书法如其人品，结字由初唐的瘦长变为方形，方中见圆，端庄雅正，气势昂扬；用笔善用中锋，有筋骨，见力度。其创立的"颜体"和柳公权的"柳体"人称"颜筋柳骨"，楷书立"楷书四大家"（另三人为柳公权、欧阳询、赵孟頫）之首，成为书法史上的一座丰碑。

义烈生成筋骨刚，端庄雅正势昂扬。
常山不屈精神在，笔下儒风与世长。

谢陆处士杼山折青桂花见寄之什
[唐]颜真卿

群子游杼山，山寒桂花白。
绿荑含素萼，采折自逋客。
忽枉岩中诗，芳香润金石。
全高南越蠹，岂谢东堂策。
会惬名山期，从君恣幽觌。

Yan Zhenqing (709—784 AD), courtesy name Qingchen, pseudonym of Yingfang, was born in Wannian, Jingzhao (now Xi'an. Shaanxi), politician, calligrapher.

During the "An Lushan and Shi Siming Rebellion", Yan Zhenqing contacted with his brother, Yan Gaoqing, and fought against the rebellion army. There were more than 30 distinguished family members passed away in the fight, demonstrating Yans' enormous integrity and loyalty. Thence, he became the Minister of the Ministry of Official Personal Affairs, Teacher of the Royal Prince, and later was conferred as the Duke of Lu Prefect and honored as the Duke of Yan Lu. Yan Zhenqing was upright, justified and courteous, not flattering, and was reputed by his righteousness and heroism. He was set up by premier Lu Qi in 784 and was appointed to visit general Li Xilie in rebellion, where he heroically refused army in rebellion and was constricted. Yan Zhenqing's calligraphy was just as his character, shape of the characters altered from the elongated in early Tang into a square, dignified elegance, momentum high-spirited style. The pen implemented sufficient usage of the center, have muscles and bones, see strength. The Yan Style created by him and Liu Style elaborated by Liu Gongquan were collectively known as "Yan rib Liu bone". His regular script was regarded as the first among the "Regular Scripture Tetra Masters"(the other three were Liu Gongquan, Ou Yangxun and Zhao Mengfu,) and a milestone in the history of calligraphy.

颜真卿撰书图

Du Fu 杜 甫

大才谁个久流离，因以艰危故蕴诗。
笔底春秋一代史，仁心可见圣人悲。

春 望

［唐］杜甫

国破山河在，城春草木深。
感时花溅泪，恨别鸟惊心。
烽火连三月，家书抵万金。
白头搔更短，浑欲不胜簪。

杜甫（公元712年—公元770年），字子美，祖辈襄阳，父徙河南巩县，先祖籍贯京兆（今长安），自号"杜陵布衣""少陵野老"（两处均指长安辖域），现实主义诗人。

杜甫出身士族，工于诗文，而生逢乱世，仕途不顺，颠沛流离，本着儒家仁爱之心，记下安史之乱后社会的一幕幕场景。其诗作题材广泛，多数反映现实，观点鲜明，尤喜描述民间疾苦，抒发其仁民爱物、忧国忧民情怀。因其诗为"诗史"，人被称为"诗圣"。杜甫诗炼字精到，意境深邃，对仗工整，在中国古典诗歌史上影响深远，并声名远播，流传日本等国。《杜工部集》（杜甫曾任剑南节度使严武幕中检校工部员外郎，简称杜工部）存诗约1500首。

Du Fu (712—770 AD), courtesy name Zimei, realistic poet, his ancestral place was in Xiangyang, Gongxian of Henan, Jingzhao (Chang' an), his pseudonyms were "Common Duling" and "Shaoling Wild Elder".

Du Fu came from the family of gentry, he was keen on poetry, and was born in an era of troublesome, during which his official career was tough and displaced. He perceived in the spirit of Confucian benevolence, noted the scene of rebellion. His poems appreciated comprehensiveness, most of which reflected realities, amongst the perspectives metaphorically depicting distinct, delineated sufferings of the people, and expressing his benevolence and worry about the country. Therefore, his poems were honored as "History of the Poems", while he was called " Saint of the Poems". The characters and words in Du's poems were elegant, deep and neat, having deep impact in Chinese classical poetical history and widely disseminated to countries like Japan and others. There are about 1500 poems left in *Collection of Construction Minister Du*.

杜甫凝思图

Lu Yu 陆 羽

平生所爱在山茶，道是人间第一花。
体悟精微留巨著，清香久沁万千家。

会稽东小山
[唐] 陆羽

月色寒潮入剡溪，青猿叫断绿林西。
昔人已逐东流去，空见年年江草齐。

陆羽（公元755—公元804年），字鸿渐，唐代复州竟陵（今湖北天门）人，号竟陵子。

陆羽博学多能，喜与名僧高士来往，善诗文，编过人物志，撰写过地方记。其后专注茶艺，对茶树栽培、育种及加工技术进行过广泛细致的考察，并擅长品茗，逐渐精于茶道。在取得茶叶生产和制作的第一手资料后，关门闭户，遍稽群书，广采博收茶家采制经验，撰写了世界第一部茶叶专著《茶经》，对中国茶业和世界茶业发展作出了卓越贡献，被尊为"茶圣"。《茶经》3卷10章7000余字，是唐代和唐以前有关茶叶的科学知识和实践经验的系统总结。

Lu Yu (755—804 AD), courtesy name Hongjian, was born in Jingling, Fuzhou(now Tianmen, Hubei) of the Tang Dynasty.

Lu Yu was erudite and talented, became friends with hierarchs, he was keen on poems and articles. He had edited the Records of the Figures and Choreographies. Later, he focused on tea ceremony: cultivation, breeding and processing techniques of tea have been widely and carefully investigated, good at tea, and gradually proficient in tea ceremony. After obtaining first-hand information on the production and manufacturing of the tea, he closed his doors, compiled a large number of books, collected extensive experience in the production of tea, and wrote the world's first tea monograph, *the Tea Classics*, which made outstanding contributions to the development of China's tea industry, and Lu Yu was honored as the "Tea Saint". *Tea Classics* conceives 3 volumes, 10 chapters, and over 7,000 words. It was the systematic summary of tea knowledge and experience in and before the Tang Dynasty.

陆羽品茶图

Han Yu 韩 愈

昌黎复古创新篇，文字清新合自然。
秦汉诗书风骨重，后人遵奉有先贤。

早春呈水部张十八员外·初春小雨

[唐] 韩愈

天街小雨润如酥，草色遥看近却无。
最是一年春好处，绝胜烟柳满皇都。

　　韩愈（公元768—公元824年），字退之，唐代河南河阳（今河南孟州）人，祖籍河北昌黎，故自称"郡望昌黎"，世称"韩昌黎"。文学家、思想家。

　　韩愈秉性刚直，敢担当，有独见，在朝敢谏，被贬有为，最大功绩在古文运动。主张继承先秦两汉的散文风骨，"文以载道"，反对追求形式而忽视内容的文风；强调道德修养、精神力量在写作中的重要作用。对唐宋文学的繁荣起了重要作用，对后世影响深远。其所创作的诗文新颖奇特，不落俗套，文字清新，述理清晰，尤其是散文在当时有着标杆性的影响。苏轼赞其"文起八代之衰"，被誉为唐代古文运动领袖，居"唐宋八大家"之首。

Han Yu (768—824 AD), courtesy name Tuizhi, was born in Heyang, Henan (now Mengzhou, Henan) in the Tang Dynasty, with ancestral place of Changli, Hebei, so he called himself "Marshall Changli", and was honored as "Han Changli", litterateur, thinker.

Han Yu was upright, temperament and outspoken, dared to speak out, perceived unique perspectives, dared to remonstrance in the dynasty, was demoted as the greatest merit in the "Ancient Scripture Movement". He advocated inheriting the prose style of the pre-Qin and Han dynasties, and opposed the style of writing which pursued form but neglects content, and emphasized the relevance of moral accomplishment and spiritual power in writing. He was significant in the prosperity of literature in the Tang and Song Dynasties and had a profound influence on the later generations. The poems and prose which he wrote were peculiar, unconventional, fresh and clear, especially the prose had an exemplary influence at his time. Su Shi praised him, and he was honored as the leader of the Ancient Scripture Movement in the Tang Dynasty and ranked the first of the " Eight Masters in Tang and Song Dynasties".

韩愈图新图

Liu Yuxi 刘禹锡

流水行云俊朗风，人间事理了然通。
身居陋室心犹趣，一代诗豪世代雄。

酬乐天见寄

[唐] 刘禹锡

元君后辈先零落，崔相同年不少留。
华屋坐来能几日，夜台归去便千秋。
背时犹自居三品，得老终须卜一丘。
若使吾徒还早达，亦应箫鼓入松楸。

　　刘禹锡（公元772年—公元842年），字梦得，唐代彭城（今徐州）人，祖籍河南洛阳。文学家、哲学家。

　　刘禹锡为王叔文革新集团的核心人物，革新失败后被贬为远州、连州刺史。奉召回京因诗再贬连州、夔州、和州等地，前后23年。刘禹锡是个哲人，被贬期间仍然积极乐观，不颓废。期间并有多篇哲学文章，最著名的是与柳宗元《天说》相呼应的《天论》三篇。由于其广泛接触社会，对民间歌谣熟悉，因此诗歌创作时常表现出清新风气。其诗大都明快爽朗，风情俊爽，充满哲人的睿智和诗人的豪情，极富艺术张力，雄浑宽广，沉着痛快，故有"诗豪"之称。

Liu Yuxi, (772—842 AD), courtesy name Mengde, was born in Pengcheng (now Xuzhou) of the Tang Dynasty, with ancestral place of Luoyang, Henan, litterateur, philosopher.

Liu Yuxi was the core figure in the Wang Shuwen's innovative party. After the reformation failed, he was relegated to Magistrate of Yuanzhou and Lianzhou. After back to the capital, he was relegated again to Lianzhou, Kuizhou, Hezhou etc. for the sake of poems, 23 years in total. Liu Yuxi was a philosopher, he was extremely optimistic during the relegation and left plethora of philosophical articles. The most famous was the *On Heaven* corresponding with *As for Heaven* of Liu Zongyuan. For the sake of his extensive contacts with the society, he was familiar with folk songs, hence, his poetry creation demonstrated a fresh atmosphere frequently. Most of his poems were lively and cheerful, amorous, full of sage wisdom and poet's pride, rich artistic tension, vigorous broad, calm and exhilarated, so he was honored as "Proud Poet".

禹锡天论图

Wang Bo 王　勃

三晋神童杨意才，文思敏捷步高台。
滕王阁上踌躇志，丽句清词逐浪来。

送杜少府之任蜀州

[唐] 王勃

城阙辅三秦，风烟望五津。
与君离别意，同是宦游人。
海内存知己，天涯若比邻。
无为在歧路，儿女共沾巾。

　　王勃（公元650年—公元676年），字子安，唐代诗人。古绛州龙门（今山西河津）人，出身儒学世家，与杨炯、卢照邻、骆宾王并称为"初唐四杰"，王勃为四杰之首。

　　王勃自幼聪敏好学，据《旧唐书》记载，他六岁即能写文章，文笔流畅，被赞为"神童"。九岁时，读颜师古注《汉书》，作《指瑕》十卷以纠正其错。曾历时三年游览巴蜀山川，创作了大量诗文。返回长安后，求补得虢州参军。在参军任上，因私杀官奴二次被贬。公元676年8月，自交趾探望父亲返回时，不幸渡海溺水，惊悸而死。王勃在诗歌体裁上擅长五律和五绝，代表作品有《送杜少府之任蜀州》。主要文学成就是骈文，无论是数量还是质量，都是上乘之作，代表作品有《滕王阁序》等。

Wang Bo (650—676 AD) was an eminent poet of the Tang dynasty. He was born into a Confucian scholar family in Longmen (now Hejin, Shanxi). He was one of the "Four Paragons of the Early Tang", the other three being Yang Jiong, Lu Zhaolin, and Luo Binwang.

Wang was brilliant and industrious as a child. According to records, he was able to write flowing prose at the age of six and was acclaimed as a child prodigy. At nine, he composed a work in ten chapters correcting the mistakes he found in Yan Shigu's annotations on *Hanshu*. He once spent three years traveling extensively within Sichuan and composed many poems and essays about his journeys. After returning to Chang'an, he obtained an official post but was later demoted twice. In August 676, he died from drowning when he crossed the sea to visit his father.

Wang excelled at writing *wulv* (five-syllable poems with eight lines) and *wujue* (five-syllable quatrains). His most famous poem was Song *Dushaofu zhi ren shuzhou* (Bidding Farewell to Curator Du as he Leaves for Duties in Shuzhou) and his most famous essay was *Tengwang Ge Xu* (Preface to the Prince of Teng's Pavilion).

王勃题序图

Yang Yuhuan 杨玉环

千般宠爱为一身，万里送荔载怨声。
可怜马嵬玉香殒，歌技舞艺后世称。

题赠张云容舞
[唐] 杨玉环

罗袖动香香不已，红蕖袅袅秋烟里。
轻云岭上乍摇风，嫩柳池塘初拂水。

　　杨玉环（公元719年—公元756年），号太真。姿质丰艳，善歌舞，通音律，为唐代宫廷音乐家、舞蹈家。其音乐才华在历代后妃中鲜见，被后世誉为中国古代四大美女之一。

　　杨玉环自入宫以后，遵循封建宫廷体制，不过问朝廷政治，不插手权力之争，以自己的妩媚温顺及过人的音乐才华，受到玄宗的百般宠爱，虽曾因妒而触怒玄宗，以致两次被送出宫，但最终玄宗还是难以割舍。公元756年，安禄山发动叛乱，杨玉环随李隆基流亡蜀中，途经马嵬驿，在马嵬驿死于乱军之中，香消玉殒。

Yang Yuhuan (719—756 AD) was known as a charming and gorgeous lady as the Imperial Concubine of Emperor Xuanzong of Tang. As a great master of both dance and music, in her lifetime Yang played the role of the imperial family musician and dancer. All these, made her enjoy the prestige as one of the Four Beauties of ancient China.

After her entering to the palace, Yang was well-behaved and never bother about the imperial court politics, let alone the power struggle. Relying on her own charm and meekness and artistic talents, Yang was exceptionally favored by Emperor Xuanzong. Although she had twice angered Emperor Xuanzong because of her envy and was sent out of the palace, Yang always kept safe and enjoyed the love of the emperor. However, in 756 , with a political turmoil produced by the Northern barbarian tribe which was lead by An Lushan, the royal couple were forced to leave Chang'an the capital. On their fleeing to Sichuan, Yang was killed because of the will of the angry soldiers. Thus, the stunner went to a tragic end.

贵妃品荔图

Bai Juyi 白居易

浮云不惑乐天然，治水苏杭造福田。
讽喻诗文补时政，幽怀长令后人怜。

赋得古原草送别
[唐] 白居易

离离原上草，一岁一枯荣。
野火烧不尽，春风吹又生。
远芳侵古道，晴翠接荒城。
又送王孙去，萋萋满别情。

　　白居易（公元 772 年—公元 846 年），字乐天，号香山居士，唐代现实主义诗人。祖籍太原，曾祖父时迁居下邽（陕西渭南），生于河南新郑。

　　白居易在上朝时频繁上书谏议时政，敢于当面指出皇上的过错。任地方官体察民情，在杭州修堤蓄水，以利灌溉。

　　白居易一生好诗，存有诗歌 3000 多首，人称"诗王"。作诗主题明确，"文章合为时而著，歌诗合为事而作"，以惩恶劝善，补察时政，因之被称为讽喻诗。与元稹共同倡导了新乐府运动。建议"立采诗之官，开讽刺之道，察其得失之政，通其上下之情。"其诗写实通俗，影响深远。

Bai Juyi (772—846 AD) was a remarkable poet of the Tang Dynasty who was characterized by his realistic style. In his career in politics, Bai persisted in his realistic style and frequently remonstrated with the government, and even dared to point out the fault of the emperor to his face. In his career as a local official, Bai had shown considerable delicacy and tact in feeling the public mood, this made him many politcal achievements. For instance, the famous programme which aimed at water storage irrigation of Westlake in Hanzhou — namely the Bai Causeway, was built by a team governed by Bai. Bai loved writing poetry all his life. Having created more than 3,000 poems, Bai was known as the "King of Poetry". In poetry composition, Bai had his strong pursuit: "the poetry is written for the happiness of a certain context, it must point out real problems of the society and the politics". By obeying this motto strictly, Bai left us a great deal of poems which were called allegory poem. In association with Yuan Zhen, a poet who enjoyed the same prestige as Bai, Bai initiated a literary reformation called New Yuefu Movement. With the friendly and down-to-earth style of poetry composing, Bai had a far-reaching impact for the later generations.

居易作诗图

Dong Yuan 董源

仁山智水育高人，溪岸疏林隐士绅。
细墨闲心描意趣，披麻一法更传真。

夏山深远
[元] 吴镇

北苑时翻砚池墨，叠起烟云隐霹雳。
短缣尺楮信手挥，若有蛟龙在昏墨。
南唐画院称圣功，好事珍藏裹数重。
崇山兀兀常疑雨，碧树萧森迥御风。
鸟啼花落不知处，渔唱樵夫退迹度。
展舒不尽古今情，未容肉眼轻将赋。

　　董源（公元934年—公元962年），一作董元，字叔达，江西钟陵（今江西进贤县）人，五代南唐画家，南派山水画开山鼻祖。

　　董源、李成、范宽史上并称"北宋三大家"，曾任南唐北苑副使，故又称"董北苑"。擅画山水，兼工人物、禽兽。其山水画初师荆浩，笔力沉雄，后以江南真山实景入画，不为奇峭之笔。疏林远树，平远幽深，皴法状如麻皮，后人称为"披麻皴"。米芾谓其画"平淡天真，唐无此品"。存世作品有《夏景山口待渡图》《潇湘图》《夏山图》《溪岸图》《平林霁色图卷》等。

Dong Yuan (934—962 AD) was the originator of the southern school of landscape painting. During his life, Dong went through a time from the Five Dynasties to the beginning of Northern Song Dynasty.

Dong Yuan, together with Li Cheng and Fan Kuan, are known as "the Three Masters of the Northern Song Dynasty". Dong was expert at painting landscape, people, as well as animals. In the history of fine arts, Dong's achievement mainly lied in his realistic description of the scenery in southern region of Yangtze River. In fact, Dong gained this achievement by his unique skill to make the painting with a visual effect of a chapped sense. The preserved works of Dong include *Photo of Xiajingshan Pass Waiting to Be Crossed*, *Xiaoxiang Painting*, *Summer Mountain Painting*, *Stream Bank Painting*, *Scroll Painting of the Forest with a Clearing up Weather*, etc.

董源写生图

Liu Zongyuan 柳宗元

不遵俗套发奇思,政见常从物态知。
迁客生涯仍卓越,纵封侯爵可如斯?

江 雪
[唐] 柳宗元

千山鸟飞绝,万径人踪灭。
孤舟蓑笠翁,独钓寒江雪。

柳宗元(公元773年—公元819年),字子厚,祖籍河东(现山西运城永济)人,世称"柳河东",唐代文学家、哲学家。

柳宗元出生于京城长安一个文化氛围浓厚的官宦家庭,受父母影响,博学刚正,有将相之才,20岁中进士步入仕途,欲展宏图做大事。哲学思想唯物创新,反对天命,远见卓识超出了同时代的学者;做学问博采众长,统筹儒、释、道,为儒、释、道三教合流奠定了基础。因参与王叔文永贞革新失败而被贬永柳,终于柳州。在柳州期间学问、政绩俱卓越。

柳宗元诗文深得骚体之真谛,平淡而奇美,为"唐宋八大家"之一,与韩愈同为古文运动领袖,并称"韩柳"。

Liu Zongyuan (773—819 AD), courtesy name Zihou, was a Chinese litterateur and philosopher commonly known as Liu Hedong in the Tang Dynasty. As a native of Hedong, he was born in present-day Yongji, Yuncheng in Shanxi Province.

Liu Zongyuan was born in a government-official family with intensified cultural atmosphere in Chang'an. Influenced by his parents, he became a promising and capable talent for his erudition and uprightness. Liu Zongyuan's civil service career was initially successful when he achieved the rank of "Jinshi" at the age of 20. His materialistic and innovative philosophical thinking, opposition to destiny and farsightedness went beyond the level of scholars in the same era. He learned widely from others' strong points and created essays synthesizing elements of Confucianism, Taoism and Buddhism, which laid a foundation for subsequent synthetization of Confucianism, Taoism and Buddhism. He fell out of favor with the imperial government because of his association with Wang Shuwen's failed reformist movement. He was exiled first to Yongzhou, Hunan, and then to Liuzhou, Guangxi. He achieved a flourishing literary and official career when he was in Liuzhou as the city governor.

For his superb writing style, he has been traditionally classed as one of the "Eight Great Prose Masters of the Tang and Song". Along with Han Yu, he was a founder of the Classical Prose Movement.

宗元奇思图

Zhao Kuangyin 赵匡胤

领兵行阵赛周郎,文以兴邦国运昌。
杯酒收权消割据,难知后世靖康殇。

日 诗
［宋］赵匡胤

欲出未出光辣达,千山万山如火发。
须臾走向天上来,逐却残星赶却月。

    赵匡胤(公元927年—公元976年),字元朗,祖籍涿郡(今河北省涿州),生于洛阳夹马营,五代至北宋初年军事家,宋朝开国皇帝,称宋太祖。

    赵匡胤出生于军事世家,勇武擅战,参与拥立郭威为后周皇帝(周太祖),典掌禁军。柴荣(周世宗)时因战功升为殿前都点检,掌握后周兵权。柴荣死后,赵匡胤"陈桥兵变"称帝,建立宋朝。而后先南后北,扫灭各地割据势力,天下一统,结束了近200年的混乱局面。赵匡胤治国重文,为防止拥兵自重发生兵变战乱而"杯酒释兵权",将各地兵权、财政权收归中央,大宋政权得以稳定,社会经济文化得以发展。

Zhao Kuangyin (927—976 AD), courtesy name Yuanlang, a native of Zhuo prefecture (now Zhuozhou in Hebei province), was born in Jiamaying, Luoyang. He was a militarist during the period from the Five Dynasties to the Early Song Dynasty. As the founder and first emperor of the Song Dynasty in China, he was referred to as Emperor Taizu of Song.

Born in a military family, Zhao Kuangyin grew up excelling in mounted archery. Later, he joined the army of Guo Wei and helped Guo to become the emperor of the Later Zhou Dynasty. Because of his brilliant combat skills, Zhao Kuangyin was promoted to a palace guard commander. Under the command of Chai Rong (Emperor Shizong of Later Zhou), Zhao Kuangyin was promoted to be a commander of the cavalry units with military leadership for his meritorious military service. After the death of Chai Rong, Zhao Kuangyin took the power by means of "Coup at Chen Bridge" and became the emperor founding the Song Dynasty. During his reign, Emperor Taizu conquered the states from the south to north region, thus reunifying most of China and effectively ending the tumultuous conditions that had last for about 200 years. In order to prevent military rebellion and strengthen his control, he lessened the power of military generals and relied on civilian officials in administration. Emperor Taizu helped reunite most of China after the fragmentation and rebellion between the fall of the Tang Dynasty and the establishment of the Song Dynasty. Military power and financial power in regions were centralized to state power to stabilize the regime of Song Dynasty so as to promote the social, economic and cultural development.

赵匡胤造像

Yue Shi 乐 史

折桂两番身世奇，生逢更代运迟疑。
读书不为功名累，留得豪情入典辞。

钟山寺
[宋] 乐史

千峰夹一径，一径花枕泉。
听泉复看花，行到钟山前。
古寺云生屋，高僧月伴禅。
自惭留一宿，区马又朝天。

乐史（公元930年—公元1007年），字子正，北宋文学家、地理学家。乐史父辈由河南迁来江西崇仁霍源（今属宜黄）。在南唐时经科考为官，入宋后再一次考中进士，先后任过著作郎、太常博士、水部员外郎及舒州、黄州、商州等地的地方官。

一生勤于著述，著书20余种，共1018卷。其中纪传体小说类对小说、戏剧发展有较大影响。其最大贡献在于编辑地理著作《太平寰宇记》，全书200卷，约130余万字，记载了北宋初各州军地理沿革及户口、风俗、人物、特产等。该书征引群书，考据精审，其体例为后代效仿，远传国外，成为一部承先启后、继往开来的划时代巨著，是研究历史地理的珍贵文献。

Yue Shi (930—1007 AD), courtesy name Zizheng, was a litterateur and geographer in the Northern Song Dynasty. Yue Shi's elder generations relocated from Henan province to Huoyuan, Chongren in Jiangxi province. He once became an official by means of imperial examination in the period of the Southern Tang Dynasty and achieved the rank of "Jinshi" in imperial examination for the second time in the Song Dynasty. He successively held the positions of the official in charge of compiling national history, Taichang Official, Ministry Councilor as well as regional officials of Shuzhou, Huangzhou, Shangzhou and other regions.

Throughout his life, he wrote more than 20 books, with a total of 1,018 volumes. His biography novel works exerted relatively important influence on the development of novels and dramas. His greatest contribution lies in the editing of geographical treatise *Universal Geography of the Taiping Era* with a total of 200 volumes and about 1.3 million words. This work recordedthe geographical evolution of regions, registered household, customs, figure and specialties etc. in the early Northern Song Dynasty. The book cited large quantities of references with a meticulous review. Its textual structure is followed by people in later generations. It is an epoch-making masterpiece and a precious literary work on the research of historical geography.

中国古代 150 位历史名人画传
ZHONGGUO GUDAI 150WEI LISHI MINGREN HUAZHUAN

乐史读书图

Bi Sheng 毕 昇

徽州自古异才乡，活字升华锦绣章。
雕刻文明因跨越，布衣工匠世留芳。

> 庆历中有布衣毕昇，又为活板。其法：用胶泥刻字，薄如钱唇，每字为一印，火烧令坚。先设一铁板，其上以松脂、蜡和纸灰之类冒之。欲印，则以一铁范置铁板上，乃密布字印，满铁范为一板，持就火炀之，药稍熔，则以一平板按其面，则字平如砥。
>
> ——[宋]沈 括

　　毕昇（公元970年—公元1051年），北宋蕲州蕲水人，巧匠，活字印刷的发明者。

　　毕昇布衣之身，传说为印刷工。时徽州读书人多，才子多，文化产业较发达，而刻版印刷难以满足出书的需要，毕昇在实践中经反复琢磨，在公元1041年—公元1048年间发明了活字印刷术。即在胶泥片上刻字，一字一印，烧硬后，便成活字，组合使用。这是印刷史上的一次飞跃，使中国成为最早运用活字印刷的国家，令文化经济的发展速度大为提高，为推动世界文明的发展做出了重大贡献。活字印刷技术被列入中国古代四大发明之一，毕昇被誉为活字印刷"师祖"。

Bi Sheng (970 —1051 AD), a native of Qishui in Qizhou, was a Chinese artisan and inventor of the world's first movable type printing technology in the Northern Song Dynasty.

Due to the relatively developed cultural industry and large quantities of bookmen in Huizhou at that time, the fixedtype engraved printing couldn't meet the demands of book printing. During the period from 1041 to 1048 A.D., Bi Sheng invented movable type printing technique based on repeated deliberation in daily practices. He used sticky clay and baked each single-type character hard in the fire for combined use of characters. It is can be said to be a leap in the history of printing, making China the first country to use movable type printing. It greatly improved the development speed of the cultural economy and made a major contribution to the development of world civilization. The movable printing technique is one of the Four Great Inventions of Ancient China and Bi Sheng is praised as the forerunner of movable-type printing.

毕昇活字印刷图

Fan Zhongyan 范仲淹

此身忧乐孰为先，楼记岳阳名世篇。
遂教书生长激励，安能蓬岛久缠绵。

渔家傲·秋思

［宋］范仲淹

塞下秋来风景异，衡阳雁去无留意。四面边声连角起，千嶂里，长烟落日孤城闭。

浊酒一杯家万里，燕然未勒归无计。羌管悠悠霜满地，人不寐，将军白发征夫泪。

范仲淹（公元989年—公元1052年），字希文，北宋思想家、政治家、军事家、文学家。祖籍邠州（今陕西彬县），生于河北真定府（今河北正定），后迁居苏州吴县。

少年时家贫而好学，常以天下为己任，《岳阳楼记》中"先天下之忧而忧，后天下之乐而乐"之名言，激励了千万有志之士。范仲淹以敢言闻名，曾多次上书批评当时的宰相，因而三次被贬。宋仁宗时官至参知政事，主持革新，提出减轻徭役、推行法制等10条建议，名"庆历新政"，成为后来王安石"熙宁变法"的前奏。范仲淹重视教育，荐拔的一大批学者为宋代学术鼎盛奠定了基础。其倡导和实践的"先忧后乐"思想是中华文明史上的一座丰碑，是中华民族的宝贵精神财富。范仲淹文学修养高，散文、诗、词均有名篇传世。

Fan Zhongyan (989—1052 AD), courtesy name Xiwen, was a thinker, statesman, military strategist, and writer in the Northern Song Dynasty. As a native of Binzhou (now Bin County, Shaanxi), Fan Zhongyan was born in Zhengding Prefecture and then relocated to Wu County .

He lived in a poor family when he was young and had taken the world as his responsibilities. "Be the first to bear the world's hardship, and the last to enjoy its comfort", the saying oft-quoted from his famous literary work *Memorial to Yueyang Tower* has served as an inspiration to the Chinese people for a thousand of years. After criticizing the Chief Councilor of the Song State when he submitted a proposal to reform criteria used in the advancement and demotion of officials for several times, Fan Zhongyan well-known for his frank proposal, was demoted to regional government for three times. He held the position of Assistant Administrator during the reign of Emperor Renzong. He uphold reform and presented a ten-point proposal (Qingli Reforms) covering various aspects of government administration, including curve reduction, implementation of legal system etc. Later, it became the prelude of Xining Reforms proposed by Wang Anshi. Fan Zhongyan emphasized education and recommended a batch of scholars, which laid a foundation of academic prosperity in the Song Dynasty. "Be the first to bear the world's hardship, and the last to enjoy its comfort", the thought advocated and practiced by him has become a monument in the history of Chinese civilization and a valuable spiritual asset of the Chinese nation. With his profound literary competence, Fan Zhongyan created large quantities of literary works including proses, poems and ci poetry etc.

仲淹忧乐图

Yan Shu 晏 殊

晏相英明善识才，知人最是在胸怀。
清词一曲倾天下，无愧当朝立辅台。

浣溪沙
[宋] 晏殊

一曲新词酒一杯，去年天气旧亭台。
夕阳西下几时回？无可奈何花落去，
似曾相识燕归来，小园香径独徘徊。

晏殊（公元991年—公元1055年），字同叔，北宋抚州临川（今江西进贤）人。文学家、词人、政治家。

晏殊14岁以神童入殿试，赐同进士出身入仕，官至同平章事兼枢密使（宰相）。为人真诚，处事公道，善识人才，唯贤是举。先后栽培推荐了范仲淹、孔道辅、王安石、韩琦、富弼、欧阳修等一批贤才，均得到朝廷重用，并有为于世。晏殊能诗、善词，文章典丽，书法亦工，而以词最负盛名。著有文集240卷，多散失。今流传词130余，诗160首，文章十篇。其词和婉清丽，意境深广，在词的发展史上，有继往开来之功，对宋代词坛贡献尤大，被人们称为北宋词家的"开山祖"。

Yan Shu (991—1055 AD), courtesy name Tongshu, a native of Linchuan in Fuzhou (now Jinxian, Jiangxi), was a Chinese statesman, poet and litterateur in the Northern Song Dynasty.

He was considered to be a child prodigy and passed the imperial examinations at the age of 14. He was bestowed the title of Tong Jin Shi and later he was promoted to Joint Manager of Affairs with the Secretariat-Chancellery and Privy Council Chief Executive (Chief Councilor). With reliance on his upright and sincere character, he developed a sharp eye for discovering able people and provided virtuous talents with equal opportunities. He successively cultivated and recommended a batch of virtuous talents including Fan Zhongyan, Kong Daofu, Wang Anshi, Han Qi, Fu Bi, Ouyang Xiu etc. They all held important positions of the imperial court and made a difference in career. Yan Shu was adept at composing poems, elegant articles as well as calligraphy. He is especially well-known for his ci poetry. During his lifetime, Yan Shu had composed over 240 collected works, but most of them were lost. Other major works in existence today include over 130 ci poems, 160 poems and ten articles. His ci poems are characterized by elegant style and profound artistic conception. In the history of the development of ci poetry, he contributed a lot to the development of ci poetry of the Song Dynasty. He is known as the "Forerunner" of the ci poetry of the Northern Song Dynasty.

晏殊识贤图

Bao Zheng 包 拯

北宋王朝用大贤，包公铁面演千年。
名臣业绩逢时运，直道清心是本然。

书端州郡斋壁
[宋] 包拯

清心为治本，直道是身谋。
秀干终成栋，精钢不作钩。
仓充鼠雀喜，草尽兔狐愁。
史册有遗训，毋贻来者羞。

　　包拯（公元999年—公元1062年），字希仁，北宋庐州（今安徽合肥肥东）人，政治家。

　　包拯少有孝行，闻于乡里；晚有直节，著在朝廷。在朝任监察御史等职时，多次弹劾权幸大臣，甚至对皇帝也敢冒犯。任开封知府时，大开官府正门，使讼者得以直至堂内见官，自诉曲直，杜绝了奸吏从中作弊的现象。包拯的执法严明，被人们誉为"铁面"，后世戏台屡演不衰，将其作为清官的化身，号"包青天"。当然，包拯能成就威名，得于皇上开明，但其自身刚正无私是主要因素。包拯在初入仕途时有诗明志，诗中有"清心为治本，直道是身谋"，其一生保持了这种品行。

Bao Zheng (999—1062 AD), a native of Luzhou (now Feidong, Hefei in Anhui Province), was a statesman in the Song Dynasty.

In comparison with his filial piety in youth, Bao Zheng is more well-known for his upright character in his old ages at imperial court. As the official in charge of the discipline of public functionaries, he impeached high-rank officials multiple times and sometimes he even dared to offend the Emperor. When he was the prefect of Kaifeng, he initiated several material administrative reforms, including allowing the citizens to directly lodge complaints with the city administrators, thereby bypassing the city clerks who were believed to be corrupt and in the pay of local powerful families. During his years in office, Bao consistently demonstrated extreme honesty and uprightness. Thus, he gained the honorific title Iron-Faced Judge". The largely fictionalized stories on "Justice Bao" have appeared in a variety of different literary forms and have enjoyed sustained popularity. Of course, the reason that Bao Zheng could establish his reputation lied in his righteous character as well as the Emperor's open-mindedness. He consistently maintained the righteous and incorruptible character throughout his life.

包公惩恶图

Ouyang Xiu 欧阳修

文忠北宋主文坛，嘉祐年间学子欢。
一榜风云龙虎会，经邦济世国之安。

采桑子·何人解赏西湖好

［宋］欧阳修

何人解赏西湖好，佳景无时。飞盖相追。贪向花间醉玉卮。

谁知闲凭阑干处，芳草斜晖。水远烟微。一点沧洲白鹭飞。

　　欧阳修（公元1007年—公元1072年），字永叔，号醉翁，北宋吉州永丰（今江西永丰）人，政治家、文学家，官至参知政事，谥号文忠。

　　欧阳修幼年丧父，随叔父在湖北长大，天资聪颖，刻苦勤奋。嘉祐二年，欧阳修主持科考，以见识取士，录取了苏轼、苏辙、曾巩、曾布、张载、程颐、程颢等一批在历史上有作为的人才，号称历史上最闪亮的一榜，影响了一代学风。欧阳修继承了韩愈古文运动的精神，是北宋诗文革新运动的领袖。其散文内容充实而简洁平易，曲折变化而流畅婉转，为"唐宋八大家"之一，后人将其与唐代韩愈、柳宗元和宋代苏轼合称"千古文章四大家"。晚年自号"六一"居士，即藏书一万卷，集录三代以来金石遗文一千卷，琴一张，棋一局，酒一壶，加自身一老翁。

Ouyang Xiu (1007—1072 AD), courtesy name Yongshu, art name Zuiweng ("Old Drunkard"), a native of Yongfeng in Jizhou (now Yongfeng, Jiangxi), was a statesman and litterateur in the Northern Song Dynasty. He once was promoted to the Assistant Councilor of the State with the posthumous title Wenzhong". Losing his father when he was young, Ou Yangxiu was brought up by his uncle in Hubei province. Apart from his in-born intelligence, he maintained an assiduous attitude toward study. At the 2nd year during the Jiayou Period, Ou Yangxiu started to preside over imperial examinations. He adopted the talent-oriented method to enroll Su Shi, Su Zhe, Zeng Gong, Zeng Bu, Zhang Zai, Cheng Yi, Cheng Hao and other capable talents. It can be said to be the most dazzling name list of Chinese imperial examinations, which exerted significant influence on academic atmosphere of an era. Ouyang Xiu revived the ethos of Classical Prose Movement initiated by Han Yu and became the leader of Poem and Prose Reform Movement in the Northern Song Dynasty. For his prose works characterized by enriched contents, explicit tactfulness, he is listed as one of the Eight Masters of the Tang and Song. Han Yu, Liu Zongyuan, Su Shi and Ou Yangxiu are jointly referred to as Four Great Prose Masters. He is also known as his art name and Liu Yi Jushi ("Retiree Six-One").

永叔举才图

Li Gou 李 觏

李觏（公元1009年—公元1059年），字泰伯，北宋建昌军南城（今江西抚州南城县）人，思想家、诗人。

李觏家世寒微，而博学通识，善辩能文，素有志于经邦济世，提出富国、强兵、安民的主张，作有《富国策》《强兵策》《安民策》各10篇。李觏不拘泥于旧说，敢于创新，成为"一时儒宗"，学子常数十百人。在政治思想方面，提出功利主义理论，反对把物质利益和道德原则对立的观点。其提出的经济理念，对王安石变法有影响。哲学上持一元论观点，承认主观来自客观，成为宋代唯物主义学派的先导。其诗歌内容大多涉及政治得失、人民疾苦。构思遣词，新颖独创，以中兴诗道自命。其《庆历民言》30篇，人称"医国之书"。

Li Gou (1009—1059 AD), courtesy name Taibo, a native of Nancheng in Jianchangjun (now Nancheng County, Fuzhou in Jiangxi province), was a poet and thinker in the Northern Song Dynasty.

Born in a poor family, Li Gou cultivated a profound knowledge and good eloquence. He had long aspired to develop social economy to help the people. He came up with the proposal of strengthening national strength, energizing military forces and ensuring people's livelihood. His works including *Strategies on Strengthening National Strength, Strategies on Energizing Military Forces and Strategies on Ensuring People's Livelihood* (comprising ten articles respectively). Li Gou didn't stick to one pattern and boldly made innovations to become the scholar of an era with many disciples. In aspect of political thoughts, he proposed utilitarianism theory to oppose the contradiction between material gain and morality principle. The economic concept proposed by him has exerted influence on the reform initiated by Wang Anshi. He held the philosophical view of monism and admitted that subjectivity came from objectivity. He became the forerunner of the materialism school of the Song Dynasty. The contents of his poems were mostly related to political losses, gains as well as common people's sufferings. He was good at verse for his ingenious creation and novel wording. His work *People's Opinions in the Qingli Period* comprising thirty articles was praised to be the masterpiece curing illness of the country.

先生本欲作良医，药国良方未得施。
潜隐盱江行教化，男儿有志尽追随。

忆钱塘江

［宋］李觏

昔年乘醉举归帆，
隐隐山前日半衔。
好似满江涵返照，
水仙齐着淡红衫。

李觏思策图

Mi Fu 米 芾

鹿门居士拜石翁，诗文书画皆精通。
流传百世不解谜，吾辈膜拜米南宫。

渔家傲·昔日丹阳行乐里
[宋]米芾

昔日丹阳行乐里。
紫金浮玉临无地。
宝阁化成弥勒世。
龙宫对。
时时更有天花坠。

浩渺一天秋水至。
鲸鲵鼓鬣连山沸。
员峤岱舆更鼇负。
无根蒂。
莫教龙伯邦人戏。

米芾（公元1051年—公元1107年），字元章，号襄阳漫士、海岳外史、鹿门居士。宋朝著名书画家。

祖籍山西太原，后定居润州（今江苏镇江），曾任无为知军。因他个性怪异，举止癫狂，遇石称"兄"，膜拜不已，因而人称"米颠"。徽宗诏为书画学博士，人称"米南宫"。米芾能诗文，擅书画，精鉴别，集书画家、鉴定家、收藏家于一身。书画自成一家，创立了米点山水。他是"宋四书家"（苏、米、黄、蔡）之一，更居首位。其书体潇洒奔放，又严于法度，为我国书家之奇才。

Mi Fu (1051—1107 AD) was an eminent calligrapher and painter of the Song Dynasty.

Mi was born in Taiyuan, Shanxi and later settled in Runzhou (now Zhenjiang, Jiangsu). Mi Fu was noted for his eccentric personality. People even called him "Madman Mi" because he was obsessed with collecting stones and even called the stones "brothers". He once served as an official professor of painting and calligraphy. Mi had a wide range of talents and was best-known for landscape painting. His style featured the use of large wet dots of ink and was called the "Mi Fu Style" by later generations. He was regarded as one of the "Four Greatest Calligrapher of the Song Dynasty".

米芾拜石图

Sima Guang 司马光

仕途失势修通鉴，卿本温文尔雅人。
一部编成资治政，求新创举赖争臣。

酬师道雪夜见寄
〔宋〕司马光

玉树交横雪后天，
银河沉着斗栏干。
笔峰微结冰丝涩，
灯晕初成花烬残。
太学先生毡苦薄，
公车倦客履仍单。
欲吟佳句到清晓，
夜寂愁闻金石寒。

司马光（公元1019年—公元1086年），字君实，号迂叟，陕州夏县（今山西夏县）涑水乡人，世称涑水先生。北宋政治家、史学家、文学家。历仕仁宗、英宗、神宗、哲宗四朝，卒赠太师、温国公，谥文正。

司马光在政治上主张对西夏、辽国采取割地忍让政策，并上《上哲宗乞还西夏六寨》。其人格堪称儒学教化下的典范。宋仁宗时中进士，英宗时进龙图阁直学士。宋神宗时，王安石施行变法，朝廷内外有许多人反对，司马光就是其中之一。王安石变法以后，司马光离开朝廷十五年，主持编纂了中国历史上第一部编年体通史《资治通鉴》。

生平著作甚多，主要有史学巨著《资治通鉴》《温国文正司马公文集》《稽古录》《涑水记闻》《潜虚》等。

Sima Guang (1019—1086 AD) was a very famous historian and politician of the Northern Song Dynasty. During his political life, Sima went through a long progress of 4 emperors' reigns including Renzong, Yingzong, Shenzong, and Zhezong.

In Sima's lifetime, the Northern Song government suffered a great threat from Xixia, a state which is in today's Ningxia province, and Liao, another state north to Song. About this situation, Sima advocated the policy of ceding land and yielding to Xixia and Liao. During the reign of Shenzong the 6th emperor of Northern Song, the remarkable prime minister Wanganshi carried out the reform policy which included using military forces to Xia and Liao. The reform was protested by many politicians, of which Sima was the most resolute one. After the failure of Wang' reform, Sima left the royal government and concentrated himself on compiling *General Mirror for the Aid of Government*, the first historical annals in Chinese history. This book, which took Sima 15years to accomplish, bestowed him a great prestige.

As a historian, Sima was very productive. Except *General Mirror for the Aid of Government*, his masterpieces include *Record of the Ancient*, *Notes on Sushui*, *To Be Low-profile and Modest*, etc.

君实编史图

Zeng Gong 曾 巩

质朴为文质朴人，身心不渝圣贤仁。
从容秀竹无华色，独占文坛一份春。

羁 游

[宋] 曾巩

粗饭寒齑且自如，
欲将吾道付樵渔。
羁游事事情怀恶，
贫病年年故旧疏。
自古幸容元亮醉，
凡今谁喜子云书。
何由得洗尘埃尽，
恣买沧洲结草庐。

曾巩（公元1019年—公元1083年），字子固，北宋建昌南丰（今江西南丰）人，后居临川。政治家、文学家。

曾巩为政七州郡，勤于政事，关心民生疾苦。整顿吏治，打击豪强，疏河架桥，兴办学校，削减公文，废除苛捐，深受百姓拥戴。

曾巩是北宋诗文革新运动的积极参与者，继承恩师欧阳修古文创作理念，文学理论主张"文以明道"，文风以古雅、平正、冲和见称。其散文温厚典雅，章法严谨，长于说理，不求文采，以自然淳朴见长，为时人及后辈所师范，列为唐宋八大家之一。

Zeng Gong (1019—1083 AD) was known as a master of prose who lived in the Northern Song Dynasty. Actually in politics Zeng also made a great contribution.

In his political career, Zeng had been in charge of seven counties. Zeng was so thoughtful and responsible to the public that during his political life he did many works, to rectify the disordered situation of local officers, abolishexorbitant tax levies, strike the bullies, dredge the river and built bridge, set up schools, and so on. All these, made Zeng win the favor of the local people.

In the field of literature, Zeng was an active participant in the reform movement of poetry and literature in the Northern Song. Zeng advocated the concept that "Writings are for Conveying Truth". The proses he composed were refined and harmonious, with strict rules and rigorous reasoning. Since his time, Zeng's proses were models for the people to learn. This made him enjoy the prestige as one of the Eight Masters of the Tang and Song Dynasties.

子固勤政图

Wang Anshi 王安石

　　王安石（公元1021年—公元1086年），字介甫，号半山，封荆国公，北宋江西临川（今抚州临川区）人。思想家、政治家、文学家。

　　王安石生于地方官家庭，自幼聪颖，读书过目不忘。从小随父宦游南北，增加了社会阅历，开阔了眼界，对宋王朝"积贫积弱"的局面有感性认识。进入仕途历任地方官，关心民生疾苦，曾上万言书，提出变革主张。拜相后主持变法，以"天变不足畏，祖宗不足法，人言不足恤"的大无畏精神推动改革，推行了一系列富国强兵措施，力图革除北宋存在的积弊。变法的意义逐渐被人们认识（尤其是近代），被誉为中国十一世纪的改革家。王安石文章节气过人，文学成就卓越，为"唐宋八大家"之一。有多篇散文、诗、词为世人称道，传之广泛。

Wang Anshi (1021—1086 AD), courtesy name Jie Fu, pseudonym Ban Shan, credited as Lord Jing, was in Linchuan, Jiangxi in Northern Song Dynasty. He was an ideologist, statesman and litterateur.

Wang was born into a bureaucratic family. He was born clever, gifted with an extraordinary retentive memory. His father, an official, brought him and visited places nationwide, which nurtured his social experience and widened his horizon. He had some perceptual knowledge on the situation of "enduring impoverishment and long-standing debility" of Song Dynasty. After he started his official career, he served as magistrate for several places and cared much for people's living. He once wrote a ten-thousand letter to the emperor, advocating the necessity of reform. After he was promoted to the prime minister, he took charge of the political reform, guided by the belief "it's no need to fear natural disasters; it's insufficient to make previous laws our laws; it's wise to ignore rumors and scandals". He bravely implemented a series of measures enriching his country and army, tried hard to eliminate the wrong doings of Northern Song empire. The significance was recognized gradually by people (especially in modern times) and Wang was credited as a Chinese reformer of the 11th century. Wang was strong-willed, and had remarkable achievement in literature. He was one of "Eight Masters in Tang and Song Dynasties". Several pieces of his articles, poems have been long and widely spread.

荆公变法地天惊，耻作中庸窃禄卿。
三不危言青史绝，丹心一片任谈评。

泊船瓜洲
［宋］王安石

京口瓜洲一水间，
钟山只隔数重山。
春风又绿江南岸，
明月何时照我还？

荆公变法图

Shen Kuo 沈 括

致政归来寻梦溪，愿将余日尽余辉。
无疆领域悠然兴，囊括前人笔下机。

开元乐

[宋] 沈括

楼上正临宫外，
人间不见仙家。
寒食轻烟薄雾，
满城明月梨花。

沈括（公元1031年—公元1095年），字存中，号梦溪丈人，北宋浙江钱塘人，学者、科学家。

沈括出生于官吏家庭，少年随父宦游各地，成年后仕途20余年，在朝为官时，支持王安石变法。曾任三司使、翰林学士及地方官，并出使辽国等，涉猎广泛，见闻丰富。晚年退休后，致力于科学研究和著述，完成巨著《梦溪笔谈》30卷，17目，共609条。其内容涉及天文、历法、气象、地质、地理、物理、化学、生物、农业、水利、建筑、医药、历史、文学、艺术、人事、军事、法律等众多领域，对许多学科有很深的造诣和卓越的成就，被誉为"中国整部科学史中最卓越的人物"，在世界文化史上有着重要的地位，西方人称之为"中国科学史上的坐标"。

Shen Kuo (1031—1095 AD), courtesy name Cun Zhong, pseudonym Meng Xi Zhang Ren，was born in Qiantang of Zhejiang in Northern Song Dynasty. He was a scholar and scientist.

Shen was born into a bureaucratic family. His father, an official, brought him and visited to places nationwide. His official career lasted over twenty years. When he once was an official in imperial court, he supported Wang Anshi's political reform. He has served as the Chancellor of San Si (three important departments), Hanlin Academician and local magistrate, and once was an envoy to Liao. Shen had abundant experiences. After he retired, he devoted himself to scientific research and writing books, and completed the great work, *Meng Xi Bi Tan* (Dream Stream Essays), of 30 volumes and 609 pieces. Its contents covered geometry, calendar, meteorology, geology, geography, physics, chemistry, biology, agriculture, water management, architecture, medicine, history, literature, art, human resource management, military, legislation etc. He had great and profound attainment in several disciplines. People credited him "the most brilliant figure in China's entire scientific history", and Shen was of great importance in world culture history. Westerners call him "the coordinate of China's science history".

沈括归乡图

Su Shi 苏 轼

书生一唱大江东，唤起豪情百代雄。
六艺精通三教彻，后人千古吊苏公。

念奴娇·赤壁怀古
[宋] 苏轼

大江东去，浪淘尽，千古风流人物。故垒西边，人道是，三国周郎赤壁。乱石穿空，惊涛拍岸，卷起千堆雪。江山如画，一时多少豪杰。

遥想公瑾当年，小乔初嫁了，雄姿英发。羽扇纶巾，谈笑间，樯橹灰飞烟灭。故国神游，多情应笑我，早生华发。人生如梦，一尊还酹江月。

苏轼（公元1037年—公元1101年），字子瞻，号东坡居士，北宋眉州眉山（今属四川眉山）人，祖籍河北栾城。文学家、书法家、画家。

苏轼乐观豪迈，才高意广，精六艺通三教，是一位历史上少有的天才。一生辗转十余处任地方官，每处皆卓有功绩。

苏轼文学、艺术多方面成就突出，堪为巨匠。其散文著述宏富，豪放自如，与欧阳修并称"欧苏"，为"唐宋八大家"之一。词开豪放一派，与辛弃疾并称"苏辛"。其诗题材广泛，清新豪放，善用夸张比喻，独具风格，与黄庭坚并称"苏黄"。苏轼亦善书，为"宋四家"之一。并工于画，尤擅墨竹、怪石、枯木等，是宋代文学最高成就的代表。

Su Shi (1037—1101 AD), courtesy name Zi Zhan, Dong Po Ju Shi as his pseudonym, was born in Meishan of Meizhou (Meishan of Sichuan province today) in Northern Song Dynasty. His ancestral home was in Luancheng of Hebei province. He was a litterateur, calligrapher and painter.

Su was optimistic, bold and generous, with great talent and high spirit and proficient in music and religion, a rare talent in history. He was official for over ten different places, wherever he made remarkable accomplishments.

Su had prominent achievements in literature, art and other realms, a real great master could he be called. Su wrote large numbers of proses, all of which showed his energetic and unconstrained feature. Ouyang Xiu and Su Shi were called "Ou Su" and they were among the "Eight Masters in Tang and Song Dynasties". As a poet in unstrained school of Song poetry, Su and Xin Qiji were called "Su Xin". His poems contained a wide range of contents, their style was fresh and unconstrained, with a brilliant use of exaggeration and metaphor. Su and Huang Tingjian were called "Su Huang". Su, good at calligraphy, was one of the "Four Calligraphers of Song". Su also painted well, especially good at painting bamboo, eccentric stones and dead wood. He represented the highest achievement of literature in Song Dynasty.

东坡赤壁怀古图

Yan Jidao 晏几道

甘居下位赏烟霞，不慕荣华酒自赊。
笔底风情融百卉，腹中童性绽千葩。

鹧鸪天·小令尊前见玉箫
[宋] 晏几道

小令尊前见玉箫，银灯一曲太妖娆。
歌中醉倒谁能恨，唱罢归来酒未消。
春悄悄，夜迢迢，碧云天共楚宫遥。
梦魂惯得无拘检，又踏杨花过谢桥。

晏几道（公元1038年—公元1110年），字叔原，号小山，北宋临川（今进贤）人，晏殊第七子，词人。

晏几道自幼潜心六艺，旁及百家，文才出众。性情忠纯，孤芳自洁不入世俗，不依权势，不慕荣华，从不利用父辈及其门生关系谋取功名，仕途不得意。

其词继承父亲风格，而因长期接触社会底层，内容丰富，思想深刻，情感真挚，艺术感染力强，雅俗共赏，使小令词在北宋中期发展到高峰，与其父同为宋词领袖，人称"二晏"。

Yan Jidao (1038—1110 AD), born in Linchuan (now Jinxian), was a poet of the Song Dynasty. He was the seventh son of Yan Shu.

Yan was known for his wide range of talents since childhood. He was of good character but was unsuccessful in pursuing an official career for refusing to use his father's connections.

Yan's poetry style resembled that of his father, being earthy and strong while restrained and elegant. Yan and his father are both revered as the leading figures of the Song poetry, and are together called the "Two Yans".

几道不慕荣华图

Huang Tingjian 黄庭坚

黄庭坚（公元1045年—公元1105年），字鲁直，号山谷道人，晚号涪翁，北宋洪州分宁（今江西修水）人，文学家、书法家。

黄庭坚自幼纵览六艺，博学多闻，是个奇童。入仕以天下为己任，为地方官仁政为民，为史官秉笔直书。后卷入党争，两遭贬谪而随缘自适，醉心文学艺术。

黄庭坚擅文章、诗词，尤工书法。早年受知于苏轼，与苏轼并称"苏黄"；诗宗杜甫。本着"文章最忌随人后""自成一家始逼真"的宗旨，矢志创新，"独立门户"，成为"三宗"（另两人为陈师道、陈与义）之一，开创了江西诗派。词与秦观齐名。书法精妙，与苏轼、米芾、蔡襄并称为"宋代四大家"。其《松风阁》诗帖遒劲苍茫，为历代行书范本。

心性当初难屈就，文章异代总相师。
诗书一派松风阁，创意三宗宋史碑。

题胡逸老致虚庵

［宋］黄庭坚

藏书万卷可教子，遗金满籝常作灾。
能与贫人共年谷，必有明月生蚌胎。
山随宴坐图画出，水作夜窗风雨来。
观水观山皆得妙，更将何物污灵台。

Huang Tingjian (1045—1105 AD), a native of Fenning, Hongzhou (now Xiushui, Jiangxi), was a scholar and calligrapher of the Song Dynasty.

As a child, Huang was famous for his genius in various areas. After becoming an official, he was benevolent and cared about the people. Later, after being demoted twice, he adapted to changes and switched attention to literature and arts.

Huang excelled at writing proses and poems and calligraphy. He was a close friend of Su Shi and they were together called "Suhuang" (a combination of their surnames). Huang was the founder of Jiangxi School of poetry and ranked as one of the "Four Masters of Song" along with Su Shi, Mi Fu, and Cai Xiang. His best-known calligraphic work was *Songfeng Ge* (The Poem on Pine Wind Pavilion).

山谷道人作诗图

Li Qingzhao 李清照

山东女子性情豪，矗立词坛泰岳高。
少妇闺中长伴枕，将军吟罢出飞刀。

醉花阴·薄雾浓云愁永昼

[宋]李清照

薄雾浓云愁永昼，瑞脑消金兽。
佳节又重阳，玉枕纱厨，半夜凉初透。
东篱把酒黄昏后，有暗香盈袖。
莫道不消魂，帘卷西风，人比黄花瘦。

　　李清照（公元1084年—公元1155年），号易安居士，齐州章丘（今山东章丘）人。宋代女词人，婉约词派代表，有"千古第一才女"之称。

　　李清照是宋代京东路提刑李格非之女，建康太守赵明诚之妻。少年便有诗名，才力华赡，逼近前辈，在当时的士大夫中已不多得，在女诗人中当推文采第一。赵明诚死后再嫁一无名氏，讼而离之。李清照晚年流荡无归，但其诗更见成就，作长短句，能曲折尽人之意，轻巧尖新，姿态百出。所谓闾巷荒淫之语，肆意落笔。自古女词人中，李清照为千古绝句之人。

Li Qingzhao (1084—1155 AD), born in Zhangqiu, Qizhou (now Shandong), was a poet of the Song Dynasty. She was widely considered as the greatest woman poet in Chinese history.

Li was the daughter of Li Gefei, an official of Song, and married Zhao Mingcheng, the local official of Jiankang. She was famous for her talent for writing poems since childhood. Her talent was thought to have surpassed many male scholars and was unparalleled among woman poets. Zhao later passed away and Li lived her later days in emptiness. Li was revered as a master of "the delicate restraint" style of Song poetry.

清照作诗图

Yue Fei 岳 飞

精忠一支岳家军，报国驱驰立殊勋。
雪耻靖康谁作主，西湖岸上祭英魂。

满江红·写怀
［宋］岳飞

怒发冲冠，凭栏处、潇潇雨歇。抬望眼，仰天长啸，壮怀激烈。三十功名尘与土，八千里路云和月。莫等闲，白了少年头，空悲切！

靖康耻，犹未雪；臣子恨，何时灭！驾长车，踏破贺兰山缺。壮志饥餐胡虏肉，笑谈渴饮匈奴血。待从头、收拾旧山河，朝天阙！

岳飞（公元1103年—公元1142年），字鹏举，宋代相州汤阴（今河南汤阴）人，军事家，南宋中兴四将之一。

岳飞少年习文练武，才智卓异，勇武过人，精通韬略，长于骑射，立志尽忠报国；青年时组织一支岳家军，纪律严明，"冻死不拆屋，饿杀不掳掠"，在抗金前线屡建奇勋。金兵称"撼山易，撼岳家军难！"岳飞欲直捣黄龙，迎回被俘的徽宗钦宗，以雪靖康之耻。因朝廷主战主和之争执，决意不明，最终被金牌召回，含冤而死，葬于西湖边。留下直抒胸臆的绝唱《满江红·怒发冲冠》，爱国激情长久地激荡在上空，昭示着后人。

Yue Fei (1103—1142 AD), born in Tangyin, Xiangzhou (now Tangyin, Henan), was a military general of the Song Dynasty.

Yue was famous for both literary and martial talents since childhood. He excelled particularly in military tactics, spearplay and archery, and aspired to dedicate his life to serving the country. He established an army with strict disciplines and won many battles against Jin forces. Yue desired to retake northern China and rescue the two former emperors of Song captured by Jin, but this was seen by the then reigning Emperor Gaozong as a threat to his throne, and sent orders to Yue recalling him back to the capital. Yue was then imprisoned and eventually executed on false charges. His tomb is located by the West Lake in Hangzhou. Yue was also celebrated for writing patriotic poems. His most widely known work was *Man Jiang Hong* (Entirely Red River), which reflects his loyalty to Song and the sorrow he felt for the nation's lost lands.

岳飞出征图

Lu You 陆　游

书剑飘零数十秋，弥留仍念同九州。
谁知马背平虏手，却在山阴道上游。

卜算子·咏梅

［宋］陆游

驿外断桥边，寂寞开无主。
已是黄昏独自愁，更著风和雨。
无意苦争春，一任群芳妒。
零落成泥碾作尘，只有香如故。

陆游（公元 1125 年—公元 1210 年），字务观，号放翁，南宋越州山阴（今浙江绍兴）人，诗人。

陆游一生主张抗金，而不断受到投降派的排斥。中年入蜀抗金，长期的军旅生活，丰富了其思想内涵。晚年回到浙江山阴老家，至死仍念抗金："王师北定中原日，家祭无忘告乃翁"。

陆游具有多方面的文学才能，尤以诗的成就为最，自言"六十年间万首诗"，今存 9000 余首。后人每以陆游为南宋诗人之冠。陆游的诗中书写了抗金杀敌的豪情和对侵略者的仇恨，风格雄奇奔放，沉郁悲壮，洋溢着强烈的爱国主义激情，思想性和艺术性都取得了卓越成就。陆游不仅成为南宋一代诗坛领袖，而且在中国文学史上享有崇高地位，是我国伟大的爱国诗人。

Lu You (1125—1210 AD), pseudonym Fangweng, was born in Shanyin Yuezhou (now Shaoxing, Zhejiang). He was a famous poet of the Song Dynasty.

Lu was a staunch advocate of fighting against the Jin invasion of Song, but was suppressed by fellow officials who wanted to surrender. He went to the Shu region (now Sichuan) to fight against Jin in middle age and spent years in military. He returned to his hometown in Zhejiang and spent his later years there. He clung to the ideal of expelling Jin forces from China all his life and was famous for writing the lines "When the day of the emperor's troops sweeping the North comes, you must not forget to tell me at my tombstone" in his best-known poem *Shi Er* (To My Son).

Lu supposedly wrote ten thousand poems, more than 9,000 of which are preserved till today. His poems were unrestrained and brimmed with passionate patriotism. He was widely considered the greatest poet of the Southern Song Dynasty and a prominent figure in Chinese literature.

陆游暮年图

Zhang Zeduan 张择端

一卷风情展宋都，千姿百态各其殊。
后人多作临摹范，难比清明汴水图。

题张择端清明上河图

[清] 玄烨

天津桥下水粼粼，
柳外盘舟夹画轮。
想见汴京全盛日，
春游多少太平人。

张择端（公元 1085 年—公元 1145 年），字正道，琅琊东武（今山东诸城）人，居住于东京（今河南开封）。北宋画家。

自幼好学，早年游学汴京（今河南开封），后习绘画。宋徽宗时供职翰林图画院，专攻界画宫室。擅画楼观、屋宇、林木、人物。所作风俗画市肆、桥梁、街道、城郭刻画细致，界画精确，豆人寸马，形象如生。存世作品有《清明上河图》《金明池争标图》（尚存争议）等，皆为我国古代的艺术珍品。

Zhang Zeduan (1085—1145 AD), born in Dongwu (now Zhucheng, Shandong), was a painter of the Song dynasty.

Zhang once served as an official painter and painted imperial buildings for the government. He was particularly good at landscape painting and was noted for capturing the details of society and the daily life of people vividly. He is most known for the masterpiece *Along the River during the Qingming Festival*, which is considered one of the greatest paintings ever in Chinese history.

择端绘卷图

Lu Jiuyuan 陆九渊

陆公求学好存疑，突破藩篱合世宜。
百虑千思终一得，能穷万物赖良知。

疏山道中
[宋] 陆九渊

村静蛙声幽，林芳鸟语警。
山樊纷皓葩，陇麦摇青颖。
离怀付西江，归心薄东岭。
忽念饥歉忧，翻令发深省。

陆九渊（公元1139年—公元1193年），字子静，号象山，南宋金溪人。哲学家、教育家。

陆九渊出生于家学渊源深厚的世家，从小好求事物根本，以存疑之心博览群书。后融合孟子的观点以及禅宗论述，提出"心即理"的哲学命题，形成新的学派——"心学"。认为天理、人理、物理只在我心中，"宇宙便是吾心，吾心即是宇宙"。强调培养学生存心、养心，以去蒙蔽而明天理，目的在于致用，即培养出能明辨是非并具有强烈社会责任感的人才。其学说对社会发展和个人成长具有启蒙作用。

陆九渊在实践中体现了其思想，知湖北荆门军，致力革除弊政，兴办实事，甚有政绩。病死于任，百姓罢市而祭。明代王守仁继承、发展其学说，称"陆王学派"，对后世哲学思想及文学艺术产生了很大影响。

Lu Jiuyuan (1139—1193 AD), courtesy name Xiangshan, was a philosopher and educationist of the Song Dynasty.

Lu was born into a scholar family, and started to read extensively and critically since childhood. Lu incorporated Mencius's thought and Buddhist philosophy and founded the School of Universal Mind. Lu emphasized the concept of mind as the source of everything including the universe and the principle. He said, "The universe is my mind, and my mind is the universe." His thought was considered beneficial to both the development of society and the growth of individuals.

When serving as the official of Hubei, Lu was dedicated to reform and promoted development, and was widely acclaimed by the people. His thought was later inherited and developed by the scholar Wang Shouren of Ming, and had a significant impact on the philosophy, literature, and arts of later generations.

陆象山正学图

Xin Qiji 辛弃疾

醉里挑灯常看剑，梦中忧患总难消。
稼轩山野闲辞赋，怎忍豪情逐水飘。

辛弃疾（公元1140年—公元1207年），字幼安，号稼轩，南宋山东历城（今济南市历城区）人。词人，爱国将领。

辛弃疾出生时，家乡山东已为金兵侵占，青年时参加抗金义军，不久归南宋。一生坚决主张抗击金兵，收复失地。任湖北、江西、湖南、福建等地官职时，认真革除积弊，积极整军备战，又累遭投降派掣肘，直至革职处分。后在江西上饶一带长期闲居，光复故国的大志雄才得不到施展，一腔忠义愤发而为词。其词句式松散而气势连贯，异于前人，独成风格，被称为"稼轩体"。作品洋溢着强烈的爱国热情和战斗精神，词风慷慨，笔力雄厚，艺术多样，而以豪放为主，与苏轼合称"苏辛"。在中国文学史上享有崇高地位，被誉为爱国词人。

破阵子·为陈同甫赋壮词以寄之
[宋] 辛弃疾

醉里挑灯看剑，梦回吹角连营。
八百里分麾下炙，五十弦翻塞外声。
沙场秋点兵。

马作的卢飞快，弓如霹雳弦惊。
了却君王天下事，赢得生前身后名。
可怜白发生！

Xin Qiji (1140—1207 AD), born in Licheng (now Jinan), Shandong, was a patriotic poet and military leader of the Southern Song Dynasty.

When Xin was born, Shandong was occupied by Jin troops. In his youth, Xin fought against Jin as a voluntary soldier for a time before returning southward.

All his life, Xin was committed to fighting the Jin forces and recovering the lost land of Song. As an official, he trained his troops hard and made preparations for war diligently, but was later slandered and dismissed. He then lived in Jiangxi in retirement. Frustrated at being unable to serve the nation and recover the lost land, his poems were noted for being filled with passion and patriotism. He was considered equally talented as Su Shi.

弃疾擦剑图

Zhao Ji 赵 佶

瘦金书体缺波澜，难应朝堂诸事繁。
国事原无文事趣，斯长彼短失江山。

声声慢·春

[宋] 赵佶

宫梅粉淡，岸柳金匀，皇州乍庆春回。凤阙端门，棚山彩建蓬莱。沈沈洞天向晚，宝舆还、花满钧台。轻烟里，算谁将金莲，陆地齐开。

触处笙歌鼎沸，香鞯趁，雕轮隐隐轻雷。万家帘幕，千步锦绣相挨。银蟾皓月如昼，共乘欢、争忍归来。疏钟断，听行歌、犹在禁街。

    赵佶（公元1082年—公元1135年），宋神宗第十一子、宋哲宗之弟，宋朝第八位皇帝，即宋徽宗。

    哲宗于公元1100年正月病逝时无子，向太后于同月立赵佶为帝。第二年改年号为"建中靖国"。宋徽宗即位之后启用新法，在位初期颇有明君之气，由于蔡京等大臣的错误诱导，政治情形一落千丈，后来金军兵临城下，受李纲之言，匆匆禅让给太子赵桓，在位25年（1100年2月23日—1126年1月18日），国亡被俘受折磨而死，终年54岁，葬于都城绍兴永佑陵（今浙江省绍兴市柯桥区东南35里处）。他自创一种书法字体，被后人称之为"瘦金体"。他热爱画花鸟画，自成"院体"。是古代少有的艺术天才与全才，被后世评为"宋徽宗诸事皆能，独不能为君耳！"

Zhao Ji (1082—1135 AD), also known as Emperor Huizong of Song, was the eighth emperor of the Song Dynasty. He was the eleventh son of Emperor Shenzong, and the younger brother of Emperor Zhezong.

Zhao was crowned emperor in January 1100 upon the death of Zhezong. He ruled for 25 years before passed the throne to his son Zhao Huan during the war with Jin. After Song's defeat, Zhao was taken captive by Jin and died at 54 after being tortured for years. Zhao was a renowned painter and calligrapher. He invented the "Slender Gold" style of calligraphy and was an avid painter of flowers and birds. He was acclaimed for his outstanding versatility as an artist and a comment goes that "Emperor Huizong excelled in all things except ruling the country".

徽宗习书图

Zhu Xi 朱 熹

少年心志作先生，选著儒家喻世声。
传承正统明官学，汇聚长河集大成。

鹧鸪天·江槛

[宋] 朱熹

暮雨朝云不自怜。
放教春涨绿浮天。
只令画阁临无地，
宿昔新诗满系船。
青鸟外，
白鸥前。
几生香火旧因缘。
酒阑山月移雕槛，
歌罢江风拂玳筵。

　　朱熹（公元 1130 年—公元 1200 年），字元晦，世称朱文公。祖籍江南东路徽州府婺源县（今江西省婺源），出生于南剑州尤溪（今属福建省尤溪县）。宋朝著名的理学家、思想家、哲学家、教育家、诗人，闽学派的代表人物，儒学集大成者，世尊称为朱子。

　　朱熹是唯一非孔子亲传弟子而享祀孔庙的人，位列大成殿十二哲者中。他是程颢、程颐的三传弟子李侗的学生，先后任江西南康、福建漳州知府、浙东巡抚，做官清正有为。官拜焕章阁侍制兼侍讲，为宋宁宗皇帝讲学。朱熹著述甚多，有《四书章句集注》《太极图说解》《通书解说》《周易读本》《楚辞集注》，后人辑有《朱子大全》《朱子集语象》等。其中《四书章句集注》成为钦定的教科书和科举考试的标准。

Zhu Xi (1130—1200 AD), born in Fujian, was a famous philosopher, educationist and poet of the Song Dynasty and was considered the most influential figure of Neo-Confucianism. He was awarded the posthumous name Wengong and was revered as "Zhuzi" by Chinese scholars.

Zhu was one of the "Twelve Philosophers" worshipped in the Confucian Temple, all other eleven being Confucus's disciples. He once studied under the Neo-Confucian scholar Li Tong. When being an official, he served in Jiangxi, Fujian, and Zhedong, and once gave lectures on philosophy to Emperor Ningzong. Zhu's most prominent work was thought to be *Sishu Zhangju Jizhu* (Collected Commentaries on the Four Books), which was set as a required reading for the civil service examinations.

朱子著书图

Guan Hanqin 关汉卿

不畏强权字汉卿，梨园碌碌诉真情。
窦娥一曲惊天地，痛彻人间冤屈声。

大德歌·秋

［宋］关汉卿

风飘飘，
雨潇潇，
便做陈抟睡不着。
懊恼伤怀抱，
扑簌簌泪点抛。
秋蝉儿噪罢寒蛩儿叫，
淅零零细雨打芭蕉。

关汉卿（公元 1219 年—公元 1301 年），号已斋（另说一斋），生于金代祁州（今河北省安国市），籍贯另有解州（今山西运城）、大都（今北京市）等说。剧作家、散曲家。

关汉卿生活在政治黑暗、社会矛盾突出的时代，由于不满于现实而不屑仕进，但其积极乐观的精神不息，一生勤奋，共著杂剧 60 多部，留下套曲 14 首，小令数十首。其作品贴切社会现实，充满血肉之感，诉说着民众的困苦与无奈，尤其将一腔悲悯，倾洒于弱势女子，最感人心魄的《窦娥冤》，传之国内外。

关汉卿杂剧内容的现实性和艺术的高超度以及数量之多，被誉为元杂剧的"鼻祖"，其散曲与马致远、郑光祖、白朴号称"元曲四大家"，并居首位，后世称为"曲圣"。

Guan Hanqing (1219—1301 AD), born in Qizhou (now Anguo, Hebei), was a great playwright and poet of the Yuan Dynasty.

Guan did not pursue an official career for discontent at the corrupt government and devoted all his effort into playwriting. He created over 60 plays, of which 14 have been preserved, and many poems. His works reflected the misfortunes of people of low social standing and were noted for depicting wretched women in particular. His most touching play *Dou'e Yuan* (Injustice to Dou E) had a worldwide influence.

Guan's plays were considered to have raised Chinese drama to a new level and placed him among the "Four Masters of the Yuan Drama", the other three being Ma Zhiyuan, Zheng Guangzu and Bo Pu. Guan was also acclaimed by many as the "Saint of Drama".

关汉卿著《窦娥冤》图

Guo Shoujing 郭守敬

修新历法世称奇，三百年间无改移。
治水司天千古典，精深数理后人追。

> 郭守敬的天文仪器，其规模和设计的精美远远超过曾在欧洲所曾看到和知道的任何这类东西。这些仪器虽经受了二百五十年的雨、雪和天气变化的考验，却丝毫无损于它原有的光荣。
>
> ——[意] 利玛窦

郭守敬（公元 1231 年—公元 1316 年），字若思，元代顺德邢台（今河北邢台县）人，天文学家、数学家、水利工程专家。

郭守敬幼承祖父郭荣家学，攻研天文、算学、水利。任同知太史院事时，奉命参与制订新历法，经过四年努力，终于编出新历《授时历》，成为当时世界上最先进的一种历法，通行 300 多年。1981 年，国际天文学会以其名为月球上的一座环形山命名。

郭守敬为都水少监时，主持修治元大都（今北京）至通州的运河。他总结了前人多次失败的原因，经细致的实地考察，制定了正确方案，完成了全长 160 多里的通惠河。从此船舶可以一直驶进大都城中，解决了运粮问题，促进了南货北销，进一步繁荣了大都城的经济。

Guo Shoujing (1231—1316 AD), born in Xingtai, Shunde (now Xingtai, Hebei), was an astronomer, mathematician, and hydraulic engineer of the Yuan Dynasty.

Influenced and guided by his grandfather Guo Rong, Guo developed expertise in astronomy, mathematics, and hydraulic engineering. When serving as a scholar-official in the court, Guo was ordered to devise a new calendar. After four years of hard work, he completed the *Shoushi Calendar* (Season-Granting Calendar), which was the most accurate calendar of the time and was used for over 300 years. In 1981, The International Astronomical Union named a crater on the Moon after him.

Guo's another major contribution was leading the construction of the Grand Canal that linked the capital Dadu (now Beijing) and Tongzhou. It allowed for grain transport and commercial interchanges between north and south of China, and played an important role in ensuring the economic prosperity of Dadu.

郭守敬修新历法图

Wen Tianxiang 文天祥

文山本是状元郎，欲挽狂澜国不祥。
困战东南碧血尽，丹心永照零丁洋。

过零丁洋
[宋] 文天祥

辛苦遭逢起一经，干戈寥落四周星。
山河破碎风飘絮，身世浮沉雨打萍。
惶恐滩头说惶恐，零丁洋里叹零丁。
人生自古谁无死，留取丹心照汗青。

　　文天祥（公元1236年—公元1283年），字履善，后改宋瑞，自号文山，南宋末吉州庐陵（今江西吉安）人，政治家、诗人。

　　文天祥出生于书香门第，21岁考中状元，历官江西、湖南等地，官至右丞相。为抗击元军，拿出自己的家产，招募壮士组建义军勤王。1276年南宋都城临安（杭州）被围，奉命与元军谈判被扣，伺机逃归，计划在闽、广重举义旗，复兴南宋。益王（端宗）在福州登位，文天祥任枢密使兼都督诸路军马，收复了赣南等地，逾两年兵败被俘。狱中三年，元军许与高官厚禄、以其妻女亲情诱迫及施以酷刑折磨等手段迫其投降，但文天祥誓死不屈，以忠烈名传后世，与陆秀夫、张世杰被称为"宋末三杰"。

　　文天祥的诗文充满忠贞气节和爱国精神，其品节如其《过零丁洋》诗，"人生自古谁无死，留取丹心照汗青"，光耀人间。

Wen Tianxiang (1236—1283 AD), born in Luling, Jizhou (now Ji'an, Jiangxi), was a politician and poet of the Southern Song Dynasty.

Born into a scholar family, Wen passed and ranked first in the imperial examination at 21. He then held several positions in Jiangxi, Hunan, etc. and was later appointed as prime minister. Being a staunch patriot, Wen once spent his family fortune on assembling a troop of voluntary soldiers to fight against the Yuan forces. When Yuan besieged Song's capital Lin'an (now Hangzhou) in 1276, Wen was sent to negotiate with Yuan on behalf of Song but was taken hostage. He later managed to escape and was appointed general of the Song army. He won many battles against Yuan but was eventually defeated and taken captive. Yuan tried lured him into surrendering but he refused and suffered for three years in prison before being executed. Wen was regarded as a symbol of patriotism and righteousness by later generations.

Wen was also noted for his poetry which brimmed with loyalty and patriotism. One of his best-known poems was *Guo Lingding Yang* (Passing the Lingding Ocean), which contains a line that goes "Since olden days, which man has lived and not died? I'll leave a loyalist name in history!"

天祥正气图

Huang Daopo 黄道婆

黄母纺织盖世技,天涯海角留足迹。
原来民间布始祖,可惜史书无半句。

黄婆婆,黄婆婆,教我纱,
教我布,二只筒子二匹布。
——民谣

　　黄道婆(公元1245年—公元1330年),又名黄婆或黄母,松江府乌泥泾镇(今上海市徐汇区华泾镇)人。宋末元初著名的棉纺织家、技术改革家。由于传授先进的纺织技术以及推广先进的纺织工具而受到百姓的敬仰。在清代的时候,被尊为布业的始祖。

　　黄道婆出身贫苦,少年受封建家庭压迫流落崖州(今海南岛),以道观为家,劳动、生活在黎族姐妹中,并师从黎族人,学会运用制棉工具和织崖州被的方法。封建正史对科学技术有着一种无知的轻蔑,再加上对下层劳动人民的顽固偏见,所以对黄道婆这样一位伟大的纺织革新家及其杰出贡献,正史没有记载,这是我国历史学的普遍性遗憾。

Huang Daopo (1245—1330 AD), also known as Granny Huang, was born in Songjiang (now Xuhui, Shanghai). She was a famous innovator of the textile industry of the Song Dynasty and was revered as the founder of China's textile industry by later generations.

Huang was born into a poor family. After she got married, she could not bear the ill-treatment from her in-laws' family and fled to Yazhou (now Haikou), where she learned spinning and weaving skills from the local Li people, who were famous for weaving the "Yazhou Quilt". She later brought the techniques back to her hometown and revolutionized China's textile industry.

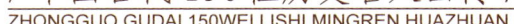

黄道婆纺织图

Wang Shifu 王实甫

一部西厢六百年，莺莺待月是天然。
元明演绎情中理，曲诵关雎子领先。

紫花儿序·也不学刘伶荷锸

[元] 王实甫

也不学刘伶荷锸，也不学屈子投江，且做个范蠡归湖。绕一滩红蓼，过两岸青蒲。渔夫，将我这小小船儿棹将过去。惊起那几行鸥鹭。似这等乐以忘忧，胡必归欤。

　　王实甫（公元1260年—公元1336年），名德信，大都（今北京市）人，祖籍河北省保定市定兴（今定兴县）。元代著名戏曲作家，杂剧《西厢记》的作者，生平事迹不详。

　　王实甫与关汉卿齐名，其作品全面继承了唐诗宋词精美的语言艺术，又吸收了元代民间生动活泼的口头语言，创造了文采璀璨的元曲词汇，成为中国戏曲史上"文采派"的杰出代表。王实甫所做杂剧，名目可考者共13种。5本21折的《西厢记》不仅是他的代表作，而且是元代杂剧创作中最优秀的作品之一。

Wang Shifu (1260—1336 AD), born in Dadu (now Beijing), was a prominent dramatist of the Yuan Dynasty. He was famous for the play *Xixiang Ji* (The Story of the Western Wing), but little else is known about his life.
As a playwright, Wang was considered to rank with Guan Hanqing. His plays had incorporated the features of Tang and Song poetry and Yuan's everyday language and featured both flowery language and vivacious dialogues. Of the 13 plays attributed to him, *Xixiang Ji*, which contained five acts and 21 scenes, is widely regarded as one of the greatest Chinese plays ever.

实甫剧作图

Huang Gongwang 黄公望

官场不顺羡山居,看破红尘作画痴。
笔墨无拘流水意,万千心绪富春知。

题 画
[元] 黄公望

茂林石磴小亭边,遥望云山隔淡烟。
却忆旧游何处是?翠蛟亭下看流泉。

　　黄公望(公元 1269 年—公元 1354 年),本名陆坚,字子久,号一峰,江浙行省常熟县人,元代画家。后过继永嘉府平阳县(今浙江苍南县)黄氏为子,居于虞山小山,因改姓黄,名公望。中年当过都察院掾吏,后皈依"全教",别号大痴道人,在江浙一带卖卜。擅画山水,师法董源、巨然,兼修李成之法,得赵孟頫指授。所作水墨画笔力老到,简淡深厚。又于水墨之上略施淡赭,世称"浅绛山水"。晚年以草籀笔意入画,气韵雄秀苍茫,与吴镇、倪瓒、王蒙合称"元四家"。擅书能诗,撰有《写山水诀》,为山水画创作经验之谈。存世作品有《富春山居图》《九峰雪霁图》《丹崖玉树图》《天池石壁图》等。

Huang Gongwang (1269—1354 AD), real name Lu Jian, courtesy name Zijiu, literary name Yifeng, a native of Changshu Prefecture in Jiangzhe, was a famous painter in the Yuan Dynasty. He once worked as a clerk in the Court of Censors in his middle age. Then, he sought for inner peace in Taoism by means of selling divinations in Jiangsu and Zhejiang provinces. He was adept at landscape paintings. He learned painting skills from Dong Yuan, Ju Ran as well as Li Cheng. He also obtained instructions from famous painter Zhao Mengfu. In painting art, he rejected the landscape conventions of his era, used very dry brush strokes together with light ink washes (when color is applied to a specific area using a soft-haired brush with wide strokes that blend them together into a unified wash) to build up his landscape paintings. "*Four Great Painters*" in the Yuan Dynasty (Huang Gongwang, Ni Zan, Wu Zhen and Wang Meng) represented the highest level of landscape painting. As was typical for Chinese scholar-officials of his era, he also wrote poetry. He also wrote a treatise on landscape painting, *Secrets of Landscape Painting*. His painting works include *Dwelling in the Fuchun Mountains*, *Nine Peaks after the Snow*, *Precipitous Mountains & Overlapped Trees*, *Tianchi Mural* etc.

陆坚观山图

Shi Nai'an 施耐庵

不恋公门处野庵，鲜明个性水云潭。
搜罗世态民间趣，塑造千年不二男。

蝶恋花·一别家山音信杳

[元] 施耐庵

一别家山音信杳，百种相思，肠断何时了。燕子不来花又老，一春瘦的腰儿小。薄幸郎君何日到，想自当初，莫要相逢好。好梦欲成还又觉，绿窗但觉莺啼晓。

施耐庵（公元1296年—公元1370年），原名彦端，字肇瑞，号子安，别号耐庵，今江苏兴化人。舟人之子，著名的元末明初作家。

施耐庵13岁入私塾，于公元1314年中秀才，公元1324年中举人，公元1331年登进士，不久任浙江钱塘县尹。后弃官归里，闭门著述，与门下弟子罗贯中一起研究《三国演义》《三遂平妖传》的创作，搜集整理关于梁山泊宋江等英雄人物的故事，最终写成"四大名著"之一的《水浒传》，被明朝皇帝看中，朱元璋屡征不应，最后居淮安卒，终年74岁。

Shi Nai'an (1296—1370 AD), a native of Xinghua, Jiangsu, was a prominent writer who lived during the Yuan and Ming dynasties.

Shi began school at 13. He later passed the civil service exams and served as the official of Qiantang County, Zhejiang. He later resigned and returned to his hometown where he focused on writing. He was also believed to be the teacher of Luo Guanzhong, author of *Romance of the Three Kingdoms*, with whom he studied and created novels together. Shi was most famous for creating the novel *Water Margin*, also called *Outlaws of the Marsh*, one of the Four Great Classical Novels of Chinese literature. He later rejected offers from the emperor for him to be an official several times and died in Huai'an at 74.

耐庵愤世图

Luo Guanzhong 罗贯中

千回百折写英雄，变幻风云一卷中。
成败是非三国演，包罗万象智谋丰。

> 良禽择木而栖，贤臣择主而事。
> 见机不早，悔之晚矣。
> ——［元］罗贯中

罗贯中（公元1330年—公元1400年），名本，字贯中，号湖海散人，山西并州太原人，元末明初著名小说家、戏曲家，是中国章回小说的鼻祖。

元朝末年，天下大乱，群雄并起，罗贯中也曾参与其中。在苏州结识施耐庵，以师徒相称，两人一同参加位于平江（即苏州）的张士诚反元起义政权，做过一段时间幕僚后离开。曾与另一位吴王朱元璋为敌，在明朝成立之后，罗贯中放弃读书人步入官场的机会，远走江南，流寓于江、浙一带，以小说抒写其"图王"霸业之胸襟，创作出代表作《三国演义》，这部长篇小说对后世文学的创作影响深远。其他主要作品有小说《隋唐两朝志传》《残唐五代史演义》《三遂平妖传》。

Luo Guanzhong (1330—1400 AD), also called Luo Ben, was from Taiyuan, Shanxi. He was a famous novelist and dramatist who lived in the Yuan and Ming dynasties.

Luo's early life saw the chaos of the late Yuan dynasty. He later met Shi Nai'an in Suzhou and became his student. They once served as the advisors of the anti-Ming leader Zhang Shicheng, but switched all their effort to creating novels after the Ming dynasty was established. Luo's most famous work was *Romance of the Three Kingdoms*, which had a profound impact on Chinese literature. His other major works include *The Chronicle of the Sui and Tang Dynasties*, *The End of Tang Dynasty and the Period of the Five Dynasties*, *The Three Sui Quash the Demons' Revolt*.

贯中述古图

Wu Cheng'en 吴承恩

无缘承受庙堂恩，洒脱逍遥浪漫魂。
着意新奇神怪事，凡尘阅尽究天门。

一叶浮萍归大海，
人生何处不相逢。
——［元］吴承恩

　　吴承恩（公元1500年—公元1583年），字汝忠，号射阳。淮安府山阳县人。祖籍安徽，因祖先聚居枞阳高甸，故称高甸吴氏。中国明代杰出的小说家，中国四大名著《西游记》的作者。

　　自幼敏慧，博览群书，尤喜爱神话故事。在科举中屡遭挫折，后补贡生。公元1566年任浙江长兴县丞。《天启淮安府志》评价他"性敏而多慧，博览群书，为诗文下笔立成，清雅流丽，有秦少游之风。复善谐谑，所著杂记几种，名震一时"。他的诗和唐代的钱起、刘禹锡、元稹、白居易不相上下；他的古文与宋朝的欧阳修、曾巩可相提并论。

Wu Cheng'en (1500—1583 AD), born in Shanyang, Huai'an, was a prominent novelist of the Ming Dynasty. He was best known as the author of Journey to the West, one of the Four Great Classical Novels of Chinese literature.

Wu read extensively as a child and was particularly interested in mythological stories. He was appointed as the local official of Changxing County, Zhejiang in 1566. According to historical records, Wu was very intelligent and well-read, and, besides being a great novelist, excelled in writing poems and prose as well.

承恩奇思图

Zhu Yuanzhang 朱元璋

起自寒微历尽艰,终生谨慎守江山。
轻徭薄赋怜民苦,更倡平民制吏顽。

咏 菊

[元] 朱元璋

百花发时我不发,
我若发时都吓杀。
要与西风战一场,
遍身穿就黄金甲。

朱元璋(公元1328年—公元1398年),字国瑞,原名重八,后取名兴宗,濠州钟离(今安徽凤阳)人,政治家,明朝开国皇帝。

朱元璋出身农家,自幼贫穷,而聪明有远见。青年时参加郭子兴的红巾军反抗元朝,以战功称王。后推翻元朝统治,统一中国而建立明朝。

朱元璋登基后节俭自守,严明法令,从谏如流。其实行的重农桑、轻赋税、兴礼乐、崇教化等革新政治、发展生产、安定民生的一系列措施,均合乎实际。尤其是在吏治方面监督严密,倡导平民反贪,百姓发现官吏违法徇私可以直接押送上司直至京城惩处。

Zhu Yuanzhang (1328—1398 AD), born in Haozhou (now Fengyang, Anhui), was a politician and the founding emperor of the Ming Dynasty.

Zhu was born into a poor peasant family, but had been intelligent and far-sighted since childhood. In his youth, Zhu joined the rebel forces and fought to overthrow Yuan. He distinguished himself as a military leader and eventually defeated the Yuan army. Zhu subsequently unified all of China and established the Ming Dynasty.

Zhu stayed frugal after ascending to the throne. He enacted strict laws and took advice from officials readily. He also instituted administrative, educational and tax reforms to improve people's livelihood and secure the stability of the country. Zhu placed a particularly emphasis on anti-corruption and allowed common people to report official misconduct to the imperial court upon noticing.

朱元璋造像

Zheng He 郑 和

郑和（公元1371年—公元1433年），名和，小名三宝，明代云南昆阳（今晋宁昆阳）人，航海家、外交家。

郑和原姓马，出生于富有冒险精神的家庭，少年入明军，在军中长大，后被燕王朱棣赏识，封郑姓。跟随朱棣，出生入死，转战南北，经历多次重大战役，有实战经验，并懂兵法，有谋略，具备军事指挥才能。被授予"钦差总兵太监"，领兵二万余航海远征，以安抚四方，稳定东南亚时局，震慑倭寇，牵制蒙、元。

先后七次下西洋，推行和平外交，传播中华文明，吸纳技术，发展贸易，完成了人类历史上文明交流的壮举。同时为国人打开了眼界，开放了思维，看到一个更为广大的天地，其意义如张骞出使西域一样，因此称海上的"丝绸之路"。

Zheng He (1371—1433 AD), born in Kunyang, Yunnan, was an explorer and diplomat of the Ming Dynasty.

Zheng was originally named Ma He. He joined the Ming army at a young age and won recognition from Zhu Di, Prince of Yan, who later became Emperor Yongle, and was conferred the surname Zheng. He fought alongside Prince Zhu Di in many battles throughout China, and demonstrated outstanding military talents. After Zhu Di ascended to the throne, Zheng was appointed as admiral and ordered to lead a naval expedition overseas. Zheng led a fleet of more than 20,000 crew members. The voyage was intended to display Ming's naval power and secure the peace and stability in Southeast Asia. It also aimed to intimidate the hostile Japan and Yuan.

Zheng commanded seven expeditionary voyages to Southeast Asia and the regions bordering the Indian Ocean. He was credited with developing peaceful relations between China and foreign countries, spreading Chinese culture abroad and bringing back foreign technology and tributes. These expeditions, unprecedented in scale, also greatly enriched Chinese people's knowledge about the world. The trade routes taken by Zheng were considered comparable to the Silk Road opened by the Chinese imperial envoy Zhang Qian to Central Asia, and were thus called the "Maritime Silk Road".

钦差七次下西洋，华夏文明播四方。
开放思维天地阔，扬帆共进启新航。

> 郑和船队在中国和世界历史上是一支举世无双的舰队，直到第一次世界大战之前，是没有可以与之相匹敌的。
>
> ——[美]路易斯

郑和下西洋图

Yu Qian 于 谦

为官清白石灰吟，历尽艰难耿耿心。
砥柱中流遭嫉妒，大明焉得不西沉。

石灰吟
[明]于谦

千锤万凿出深山，
烈火焚烧若等闲。
粉身碎骨全不怕，
要留清白在人间。

于谦（公元1398年—公元1457年），字廷益，号节庵，明朝浙江钱塘县人。政治家、军事家。

于谦性情淳朴忠厚，一生为官清廉，重名节，轻名利；重成仁，轻杀身；重社稷，轻君王。巡按江西，雪冤案数百件。巡抚河南、山西，深入里巷赈济灾荒，将镇将私垦的田收为官屯，以补边防军需。明英宗被俘时，拥立景帝，调集各路军马严守京城。主持兵部工作时，北部敌寇势力正扩张，南部各自拥兵自封，西南等地作乱，于谦逐一安排应对。英宗被释，于谦说服景泰帝接英宗归来。后反受诬告被处死，抄家时发现其家无余财。

Yu Qian (1398—1457 AD), born in Qiantang, Zhejiang, was a politician and general of the Ming Dynasty.

Yu was famous for his uprightness and loyalty to Ming. When serving as the governor of Jiangxi, he was said to have corrected hundreds of unjust verdicts. When he governed Henan and Shanxi, he led the relief of famine and confiscated the farmland embezzled by local officials to supply food to the defending troops at the border. When Emperor Yingzong was captured and held hostage by the Mongol armies, Yu placed the Emperor Jingtai on the throne and led the defense of the capital. He was also credited with suppressing revolts and maintaining the peace of China. However, when Emperor Yingzong was released and returned to the throne, Yu was falsely accused of treason and sentenced to death.

于谦造像

Wang Shouren 王守仁

文能益世传中外，武有奇谋破敌顽。
五百年间难再遇，知行合一启人寰。

三山晚眺
[明] 王守仁

南望长沙香霭中，鹅羊只在暮云东。
天高双橹哀明月，江阔千帆舞逆风。
花暗渐惊春事晚，水流应与客愁穷。
北飞亦有衡阳雁，上苑封书未易通。

　　王守仁（公元1472年—公元1529年），字伯安，别号阳明。明代浙江余姚人，思想家、哲学家、文学家和军事家。

　　王守仁出身于书香门第、官宦世家，父亲状元，随父宦游，见多识广，少年能诗。历任知县、巡抚、总督等职，官至南京兵部尚书，以平定江西之乱，封新建伯（后追加为侯），谥文成，故又称王文成公。

　　王守仁精通儒、道、佛，是陆王心学之集大成者。其主张"心外无理""知行合一"，以对抗程朱学派割裂知行关系的观点。其学说以"反传统"的姿态出现，在明代中期以后，形成了阳明学派，弟子极众，远传日本、朝鲜半岛及东南亚。后人誉其集立德、立功、立言于一身，成就冠绝明代。

Wang Shouren (1472—1529 AD), also known as Wang Yangming, born in Yuyao, Zhejiang, was a thinker, philosopher, scholar and military leader of the Ming Dynasty.

Wang was born into a scholar-official family. He was well educated by his father, who was scholarly and once ranked first at the imperial examination. He later served in many important positions and was made Earl of Xinjian for suppressing peasant revolts in Jiangxi. His posthumous name was Wencheng.

Wang was a leading figure in the School of Mind. He developed the idea of "innate knowing" and advocated integration of knowledge and action. His thought became popular in China and was influential in Japan, Korea, and South-east Asia. Wang was regarded by many the greatest thinker of the Ming Dynasty.

阳明三立图

Wang Gen 王 艮

下层奔走苦思寻,圣道当符百姓心。
兴学泰州传道广,启蒙时代一强音。

次韵风月亭留题
[明]王艮

重来扬子故人远,满目风烟如隔生。
我游无往不适意,世故何者能关情。
清宵宴坐山月上,白日缓步江风轻。
扁舟欲发更留滞,隔岸杳杳来钟声。

  王艮(公元1483年—公元1541年),字汝止,号心斋。明代泰州安丰场(今江苏东台)人,哲学家。

  王艮7岁入乡塾,11岁因家贫辍学,随父兄制盐。因随父经营至山东拜谒孔庙得启发,于是发奋读书。十数年后,家为富户,遂专心求学。中年拜任职江西的王守仁为师,经王守仁点化转而治学,创立了传承阳明心学的泰州学派。主张以"安身立本"为伦理道德的出发点,强调身为天下国家的根本;宣传"百姓日用即道""百姓日用之学"及"正人必先正己""正身应人人平等"的观点;重视人的自身价值和个人的社会权利。泰州学派对后世思想、哲学、文学戏剧等影响很大。

Wang Gen (1483—1541 AD), a native of Taizhou (now Dongtai, Jiangsu), was a philosopher of the Ming Dynasty.

Wang started school at seven but dropped out at eleven because of poverty. He then helped his father and older brother make and sell salt. It was said that he was inspired when visiting a Confucian temple and started to study diligently. He was later accepted by the great philosopher Wang Shouren as a disciple. Wang was known for establishing the Taizhou school, which advocated human rights and equity. His thought was considered to have a profound impact on Chinese philosophy and literature.

王艮思道图

Hai Rui 海 瑞

世代都夸海瑞忠，上疏强谏入囚笼。
耿介甘心生计苦，最难家小亦贫穷。

吴人姜谥

[明] 海瑞

海父真人杰，三朝第一臣。
寸心惟为主，百计只安民。
折槛彰忠迹，埋轮雠佞人。
最怜贫与独，青史泪痕新。

海瑞（公元1514年—公元1587年），字汝贤，自号刚峰，明代琼山（海南海口）人，政治家。

海瑞幼年丧父，孤儿寡母，生活贫苦，自幼立志要当清官。入仕后在浙江淳安和江西兴国等地，推行清丈田地、平赋税，平反冤案，打击贪官污吏，深得民心。任户部主事时，自备棺木冒死上书，批评世宗迷信巫术、生活奢华、不理朝政等弊端，被捕入狱。世宗死后获释复官，一如既往，刚正不阿，惩治贪官，打击豪强，强令贪官豪强退田还民。后被排挤，革职闲居16年，再被起用，两年后病逝。死时家无余钱，无后嗣，家具破旧，赖同事捐资以葬。赠太子太保，谥忠介。海瑞一生清廉正直，深得民众尊崇，被誉为"海青天"。

Hai Rui (1514—1587 AD), born in Qiongshan (now Haikou, Hainan), was a celebrated official of the Ming Dynasty.

Hai's father died when he was little and he was raised by his mother. He aspired to be a upright official since childhood. After beginning his official career, he served as local officials in Zhejiang and Jiangxi. He gained a reputation for his upright morality, honesty, frugality, and fairness. This won him widespread popular support but made him many enemies in the bureaucracy. He was later appointed chief official of the Ministry of Revenue at the Imperial Court. He was sent to prison for strongly criticizing the Jiajing Emperor for the neglect of his duties and engaging in superstitious activities. He was released after the Emperor died and was reappointed by Emperor Longqing. He was later forced to resign and spent 16 years in retirement before being appointed again. He died two years later. Hai's honesty and uprightness earned him the name "Hai Qingtian", which means an incorruptible official.

海瑞造像

Li Shizhen 李时珍

遍踏山川觅处方，穷搜典籍辨毫芒。
亲尝百草神农继，秘籍全书世界扬。

> 性理之精蕴，格物之通典，帝王之秘籍，臣民之重宝。
>
> ——［明］王世贞

　　李时珍（公元1518年—公元1593年），字东璧，明代湖北蕲春县人，医药学家。

　　李时珍出生于行医世家，小时体弱多病，然性格坚强，对八股文无兴趣，放弃科举，专心学医。曾任太医院判一年，便辞职回乡。先后27年深入名山大川、都市乡村收集药物标本和处方，并拜渔人、樵夫、农民、车夫、药工、捕蛇者为师，参考了历代医药等方面书籍925种，考古证今、穷究物理，做了上千万字札记，完成了巨著《本草纲目》。全书192万字，含药物1892种，药方11096则，附药物形态图1100余幅，成为当时最系统、最完整、最科学的一部医药学著作，不仅为中国药物学的发展作出了重大贡献，而且对世界医药学、植物学、动物学、矿物学、化学的发展也产生了深远的影响，被誉为"东方医药巨典"。

Li Shizhen (1518—1593 AD), born in Qichun, Hubei, was a pharmacologist of the Ming Dynasty.

Li was born into a doctor family. When he was little, he constantly fell ill but was strong-willed. He was uninterested in studying for the civil service exams and focused on studying medicine. He once got a position at the Imperial Medical Institute but resigned a year later and returned home. Li was famous for his scientific masterpiece *Compendium of Materia Medica*, the writing of which took him altogether 27 years. In the writing of the book, Li travelled extensively, collecting herbs and remedies and interviewing peasants, hunters, fishermen, and lumberjacks. He consulted over 925 medical books and his notes contained over ten million characters. *Compendium of Materia Medica* contains a total of 1,920,000 characters. It containng 1,892 drugs, 11,096 prescriptions, and 1,100 illustrations, was regarded the most complete and comprehensive medical book at the time. It had a profound impact on subjects including botany, zoology, mineralogy, and chemistry.

时珍觅药图

Feng Xiaoqing 冯小青

自幼聪颖赋新词，音律奕棋惊世时。
误入武林富豪家，瘦影自临春水池。

怨
[明] 冯小青

新妆竟与画图争，
知是昭阳第几名？
瘦影自临春水照，
卿须怜我我怜卿。

　　冯小青（生卒年不详），中国著名才女、词人。自小秀丽聪颖，孤芳自怜。据清初《女才子书》中记载，本名玄玄，明晚期人，大致生于万历晚期，其事迹记于张岱《西湖梦寻》之《小青佛舍》一篇：小青，广陵人。十岁时遇老尼，口授《心经》，一过成诵。尼曰：是儿早慧福薄，乞付我作弟子。而母亲不许。小青好读书，解音律，善弈棋。但误落武林富人，为其小妇，遭大妇奇妒，百般凌逼。小青整天与《西厢记》《牡丹亭》为伴，十八岁时抑郁而殒，生前将其诗稿焚烧一尽。

Feng Xiaoqing was a noted poet who supposedly lived in the late Ming Dynasty. Legend has it that she met a Buddhist nun at the age of ten who, impressed by Feng's retentive memory, wished to take her as a disciple. But Feng's mother rejected. Feng loved reading books and was good at music and playing go. She later became the concubine of a rich man but was bullied by the man's wife. She thus spent most of her time reading books to dispel her sorrow. She was said to have burnt all her manuscripts before she died of depression at 18.

冯小青造像

Li Zhi 李 贽

鉴古观今见识深，王朝不许异端音。
通身是胆通州逝，难锁自由求索心。

独 坐
[明] 李贽

有客开青眼，无人问落花。
暖风熏细草，凉月照晴沙。
客久翻疑梦，朋来不忆家。
琴书犹未整，独坐送残霞。

　　李贽（公元1527年—公元1602年），初姓林，名载贽，后改姓李，名贽，字宏甫，号卓吾，别号温陵居士等，明代福建泉州人，思想家、文学家。

　　李贽出生于教师家庭，喜读书究学问。入仕后历教谕、国子监博士、知府等20余年。其为官的准绳是"一切持简易，任自然，务以德化"，自甘清苦。李贽曾师泰州学派的学者王襞（bì，王艮的儿子），与王艮弟子罗汝芳等志同道合，继承泰州学派思想，成一代宗师。主张"绝假还真、真情实感"的"童心说"，批判程朱理学的虚伪，反对封建礼教的禁锢；同情百姓疾苦，主张个性自由；批判重农抑商，倡导功利价值；直至抨击时政，针砭时弊。公然宣称自己的著作是"离经叛道之作"。后被诬"异端邪说"囚于通州，死于狱。其学说符合明中后期资本主义萌芽的发展要求，对晚明思想文学有着重要影响。

Li Zhi (1527—1602 AD), a native of Quanzhou, Fujian, was a philosopher and writer of the Ming Dynasty.

Li was born into a teacher's family and loved reading and studying. As an official, he served in different positions for over 20 years and maintained a frugal lifestyle. Li was influenced by the Taizhou School and was a critic of the Cheng-Zhu School. He advocated that people should have the freedom to express their personalities and became known as a representative of anti-feudal thought. He was later charged with spreading deviant opinions and was persecuted and died in prison. His ideas were considered to be in line with the then emerging capitalism thought and to have significant influence on the philosophy and literature of the late Ming Dynasty.

卓吾针砭时弊图

Qi Jiguang 戚继光

闽南蓟北马匆匆，四十年间抗寇凶，
锐器精兵震敌胆，威名激荡国人风。

望阙台

[明] 戚继光

十年驱驰海色寒，
孤臣于此望宸銮。
繁霜尽是心头血，
洒向千峰秋叶丹。

　　戚继光（公元1528年—公元1588年），字元敬，号南塘，晚号孟诸，卒谥武毅，山东蓬莱人（一说祖籍安徽定远，生于山东济宁微山县鲁桥镇）。明朝抗倭名将，杰出的军事家、书法家、诗人。

　　戚继光在东南沿海抗击倭寇十余年，扫平了多年为虐沿海的倭患，确保了沿海人民的生命财产安全；后又在北方抗击蒙古部族内犯十余年，保卫了北部疆域的安全，促进了蒙汉民族的和平发展。写下了十八卷本《纪效新书》和十四卷本《练兵实纪》。

　　同时，戚继光又是一位杰出的兵器专家和军事工程家，他改造、发明了各种火攻武器；他建造的大小战船、战车，使明军水路装备优于敌人；他富有创造性地在长城上修建空心敌台，进可攻，退可守，是极具特色的军事工程。

Qi Jiguang (1528—1588 AD), was born in Penglai, Shandong. He was a military strategist, calligrapher and poet of the Ming Dynasty. He is best known for leading the defense on the coastal regions against Japanese pirates.

Qi fought against the Japanese pirates on the southeast coast of China for more than ten years. He subsequently fought against the Mongol tribes and maintained peace in northern China. He also helped improve the relation between the Mongols and the Han people. He wrote two books on *military strategy* – *Jixiao Xinshu* (New Treatise on Military Efficiency) and *Lianbing Ji* (Record of Military Training).

Qi Jiguang was also an outstanding weapon expert and military engineer. He improved and invented many weapons and was known for directing the construction of watchtowers along the great wall.

继光抗倭图

Tang Xianzhu 汤显祖

还魂一曲话情殇，肠断娄江俞二娘。
若士非为情所累，或将情梦喻官场。

秋日西池望二仙桥
［明］汤显祖

池上映秋光，登临爱夕阳。
镜中蒲柳色，衣上芰荷香。
听雨初留屐，当风一据床。
猗兰延客语，高菊以邻芳。
紫翠连山暝，晴阴隔水凉。
坐看人世小，仙驭白云乡。

汤显祖（公元1550年—公元1616年），字义仍，号若士、清远道人，明代临川人，戏曲家、文学家。

汤显祖出身于书香门第之家，学问涉猎广，古文诗词颇精，通天文地理、医药卜筮。曾师于罗汝芳，受泰州学派影响，崇尚心灵自由。入仕后历任太常寺博士、詹事府主簿、礼部祠祭司主事。因揭发时政积弊，抨击朝廷，而被谪广东徐闻典史，后调任浙江遂昌知县。为官体恤民情，深得民心，受排挤回乡，专心编写戏剧。取古代传奇小说改编了《牡丹亭》《紫钗记》《南柯记》《邯郸记》四部戏剧，合称"临川四梦"。其中以《牡丹亭》影响最大，其情生情死的剧情，表达了汤显祖冲破封建伦理束缚、追求自由的理想，隐喻了他对当时官场腐败的愤懑之情。

Tang Xianzu (1550—1616 AD), a native of Linchuan, was a playwright of the Ming Dynasty.

Tang was born into a scholar family, and studied a wide range of subjects including literature, astronomy, geography and medicine. He was once a student of Luo Rufang. Influenced by the Taizhou School, Tang was an advocate of inner freedom. He worked as an official in different positions for a time but was later dismissed. He then returned to his hometown and focused on playwriting. His four major works, namely *The Peony Pavilion*, *The Purple Hairpin*, *Record of Southern Bough*, and *Record of Handan*, are collectively called the "Four Dreams of Linchuan", among which *The Peony Pavilion* is generally considered his greatest play. It narrated a tortuous love story and was considered to reflect Tang's desire for freedom and resentment at the corrupt official system.

若士说戏图

Xu Guangqi 徐光启

平生所好在经营，总览诸家农政声。
勘误存真遗产荟，谦谦一片利民情。

大赞诗
[明] 徐光启

维皇大哉，万汇原本；巍巍尊高，
造厥胚浑。抟捖众有，以资人灵；
无然方命，悉尔所生。蠢蠢黔首，
云何不淑？曾是群瞢，上惉下黩。
帝曰悯斯，降于人间；津梁耳目，
卅有三年。普拯横流，诞彰神奇；
舍尔灵躯，请命作仪。粤有圣宗，
十又二子；述宣宏化，以迨亿祀。
如日之升，逾远而光。千六百载，
达于兹方。兹方云何？膺受多祜。
正教西来，大眷东顾。凡我人斯，
仰瞻辽廓。敢曰无主，敢曰不若？
大文无雕，经涂无诡。秉心三德，
守诚二五。若冈不升，违冈不坠。
勖矣前修，无作后悔。后悔则那，
亟其改辙。鉴尔一息，赀尔百年。
如山匪岿，如海匪渊。矢志崇闳，
以隆德馨。

徐光启（公元1562年—公元1633年），字子先，明代松江府（今上海市徐家汇）人，科学家、政治家。

徐光启出生于农商兼营的家庭，从小爱探讨农业知识，生平务经世实用之学，入仕后官至礼部尚书兼文渊阁大学士，为朝中重臣，政务繁忙仍坚持究学，考证著述。在天文、数学、历法、水利、农业、军事等方面均有成就，而以农学为最。其《农政全书》12目，共60卷，50余万字，包括农本、田制、农事、水利、农器、树艺、蚕桑、牧养、制造、荒政等，囊括了中国古代汉族农业生产和人民生活的各个方面，是一部集前人之大成的农业百科全书。

徐光启十分重视国外先进文化，将国外最新科技知识采编入著，还和利玛窦一起译出了希腊欧几里得的数学原理名著《几何原本》并出版，是我国中西文化科技交流的先驱者。

Xu Guangqi (1562—1633 AD), born in Songjiang (now Shanghai), was a scientist and politician of the Ming Dynasty.

Born into a peasant-merchant family, Xu was interested in agriculture and applied science since childhood. He later served as the chief official of Ministry of Rites and Grand Secretary of Wenyuan Hall. Xu continued conducting researches and writing works when being an official, and made achievements in a wide range of areas, among which his achievements in agricultural science stood out.

His work *Nong Zheng Quan Shu* (Complete Treatise on Agriculture), containing 60 volumes and more than 500,000 characters, was a comprehensive encyclopedia on Chinese agriculture.

Xu was also noted for translating Euclid's *Elements* into Chinese in collaboration with Matteo Ricci, and was the first of Chinese to promote cross-cultural communication between China and the western world.

明礼部尚书徐光启造像

Feng Menglong 冯梦龙

冯公警世著三言，体己为民净六根。
理范情维尘俗道，创新大汉文化园。

醒世恒言
［明］冯梦龙

富贵本无根，尽从勤里得。
请观懒惰者，面待饥寒色。

冯梦龙（公元1574年—公元1646年），字犹龙，又号墨憨斋主、顾曲散人、吴下词奴等，明代南直隶苏州府（今江苏苏州）人，文学家、戏曲家。

冯梦龙出身名门世家，从小好读书，原欲应试入仕，然屡试不中，因热恋一歌妓，于茶坊酒楼频繁接触下层社会，积累了民间文学第一手资料。至58岁才入仕，61岁为寿宁县令，4年后回乡，仍旧读书著述。70岁高龄，奔走呼吁反清，刊行《中兴伟略》。其虽有经世治国之志，但又不愿受封建道德的约束，思想上受王守仁、李贽影响，强调真挚的情感，反对虚伪的礼教。主张以"情教"取代"宗教"，认为文学的教化作用，可以净"六更"，去杂念，比说教更有益于社会。著有《喻世明言》《警世通言》《醒世恒言》，皆盛传于世，是中国白话短篇小说的经典代表作，创新、丰富了汉文学。

Feng Menglong (1574—1646 AD), born in Suzhou, Jiangsu, was a scholar and writer of the Ming Dynasty.

Feng was born into an eminent family and loved reading books since childhood. He failed to pass the civil service examinations several times and spent most of his early days with middle and working class people. He collected substantial first-hand materials on Chinese folk literature during those years. He started his official career at 58 and served as the magistrate of Shouning County. He returned to his hometown four years later and lived out his days reading and writing books. He joined the anti-Qing campaign later at the age of 70. Feng advocated that people be true to their genuine feelings and believed that literature works could shape people's character better than preaching. His works include *Yushi Mingyan* (Illustrious Words to Instruct the World), *Jingshi Tongyan* (Stories to Caution the World) and *Xingshi Hengyan* (Stories to Awaken the World), all considered classics of Chinese vernacular novels. Feng's works are also thought to have innovated and enriched Chinese literature.

墨憨斋主梦龙发奋图

Xu Xiake 徐霞客

羡尔行囊走四方，无忧有胆任荒凉。
探幽寻秘奇文记，立志难能若此刚。

薄海内外，无如徽之黄山。登黄山，天下无山，观止矣！

——[明] 徐霞客

徐霞客（公元 1587 年—公元 1641 年），名弘祖，字振之，号霞客，明代江苏江阴人，地理学家、探险家、旅行家和文学家。

徐霞客祖辈读书，其父不愿为官，喜游山水。徐霞客受父亲影响，博览图经地志游记，立志遍游名山大川。22 岁时，背上行囊，离开了家乡，先后走过 19 省，直到 54 岁逝世，绝大部分时间都是在旅行考察中度过。在风餐露宿中，每晚记下见闻，共 260 多万字，经整理出 60 多万字的《徐霞客游记》。其游记开辟了地理学上系统考察描述自然的新思路，纠正了古代流传的一些谬误（如长江起源）。其考察之广和研究之深，在世界地理学史上空前。该书既是系统考察祖国地貌地质的地理名著，又是描绘华夏风景资源的旅游巨篇，还是文字优美的文学佳作，在国内外具有深远的影响。徐霞客被称为"千古奇人"，其作开篇之日（5 月 19 日）被定为中国旅游日。

Xu Xiake (1587—1641 AD), also known by his birth name Xu Hongzu, was born in Jiangyin, Jiangsu. He was a geographer, explorer, and travel writer of the Ming Dynasty.

Xu was born into a scholar family. Influenced by his father, Xu read a lot of travel records as a child and aspired to travel throughout China. He started his first journey at 22 and spent most of his life travelling and writing travel records. He journeyed through 19 provinces before he died at 54. He compiled his records into his best-known work *Xu Xiake Youji* (Travel Diaries of Xu Xiake), which was a groundbreaking book in the history of geography. The book provides detailed accounts of China's topography and is also considered to be of great literature value. May 19, the date when Xu began writing this masterpiece is now commenmorated as China's National Tourism Day.

霞客游记图

Song Yingxing 宋应星

立心唯物尚天然，顺应潮流继古贤。
绩学先从功效始，若无高雅怎空前。

怜愚诗

[明] 宋应星

一个浑身有几何？学书不就学兵戈。
南思北想无安着，明镜催人白发多！

宋应星（公元 1587 年—公元 1666 年），字长庚，明末江西奉新人，科学家。

宋应星出身于书香门第之家，从小读书过目不忘，经多次入京会试不中，受张载的唯物主义自然观影响，立志"为往圣继绝学"，为民生究实用之术，因致力于对农业和手工业生产的科学考察和研究，收集了丰富的科学资料，经日夜刻苦钻研，完成《天工开物》。全书分为上、中、下三篇 18 卷，附有 123 幅插图，描绘了 130 多项生产技术和工具的名称、形状、工序，记载了明朝中叶以前中国古代农业、手工业制造等各项技术，被誉为"中国 17 世纪的工艺百科全书"。此书顺应了当时商品经济发展和生产技术进步要求。这种尊重自然规律、立足民生需要的做法，永远值得人们学习。宋应星后为官福建汀州、安徽亳州，明亡后弃官，誓不出仕，终老乡里。

Song Yingxing (1587—1666 AD), a native of Fengxin, Jiangxi, was a scientist of the late Ming Dynasty.

Song was born into a scholar family and was said to have exceptional memory as a child. After failing the imperial examinations several times, he switched his interest to applied sciences and technologies. He was best-known for his work *Tiangong Kaiwu* (The Exploitation of the Works of Nature), an encyclopedia comprising 18 chapters and 123 illustrations. The work records over 130 production processes and tools and covers a wide range of technical issues about ancient China's agriculture and manufacturing industry. Song's work is widely revered in China and is thought to be of practical use to the development of society. Song served as an official in Fujian and Anhui. After the fall of Ming, he resigned and vowed to never hold an official post again. He lived out his life in his hometown.

应星天工开物图

Shi Kefa 史可法

推论扬州十日屠，若从强敌节已疏。
成仁取义孤忠愤，不负当年立誓初。

六安署病中感怀

［明］史可法

待理犹烦苦抱疴，公余侧枕奈如何？
民饥由己嗟艰食，兵悍逢人欲弄戈。
抚字无能先布德，催科宁忍复为苛。
白云交瘁燕山下，国手谁怜妙剂多？

史可法（公元 1601 年—公元 1645 年），字宪之，号道邻，明末河南祥符人，祖籍顺天府（北京），军事家。

史可法少年以孝行闻名，师从名臣左光斗，继其忠义之心。入仕后，随名将卢象升转战各地平叛，后任兵部尚书、礼部尚书兼东阁大学士。1644 年北京被攻陷后，拥立福王于南京。在内乱外患之时，曾欲与清军议和，以先除内乱。1645 年，清军大举南犯，史可法督战扬州，顽强抗敌，拒绝多尔衮多次劝降，城破身亡。清军伤亡重，怒屠扬州 10 日。南明朝廷谥之为"忠靖"。后乾隆帝称道史可法之忠烈追谥为"忠正"。后人收其著作，编为《史忠正公集》。

Shi Kefa (1601—1645 AD) was a native of Xiangfu, Henan. He was a military strategist of the late Ming Dynasty.

When he was young, Shi was famous for fulfilling filial duties and was mentored by a celebrated official named Zuo Guangdou. He later fought along with the general Lu Xiangsheng to suppress revolts and was appointed the chief official of the Ministry of War. When the Qing troops overthrew Ming and seized control of Beijing in 1644, Shi supported the Prince of Fu, a descendant of the Ming imperial family, as emperor and helped establish a new capital in Nanjing. In 1645, Qing forces marched southward and Shi led the defense of Yangzhou. He fought tenaciously and was killed when Yangzhou fell to Qing forces.

After his death, the Ming dynasty granted him the posthumous name "Zhongjing" and later Emperor Qianlong of Qing granted him another posthumous name "Zhongzheng". His descendants collected his works and compiled them into *Shi Zhongzheng Gong Ji* (Collected Works of Shi Zhongzheng).

可法督战图

Gu Yanwu 顾炎武

山河痛惜久沉沦，天下之忧最是贫。
民族复兴民有责，诗文徒尔湿纱巾。

海上 其一
[明] 顾炎武

南营乍浦北南沙，终古提封属汉家。
万里风烟通日本，一军旗鼓向天涯。
楼船已奉征蛮敕，博望空乘泛海槎。
愁绝王师看不到，寒涛东起日西斜。

顾炎武（公元1613年—公元1682年），本名绛，字忌清，后改名炎武，明末清初苏州昆山人，思想家、经学家、史地学家和音韵学家。

顾炎武出生于望族，青年时发愤为经世致用之学，未能入仕，深感八股文之害。清军南下后，言"天下兴亡，匹夫有责"，参加抗清义军，结诗社，秘密进行抗清活动，探索"国家治乱之源，生民根本之计"，并从"明道救世"的经世思想出发，大胆怀疑君权，提出反对"独治"，主张"众治"的观点。

顾炎武学问渊博，对于国家典制、郡邑掌故、天文仪象、河漕、兵农及经史百家、音韵训诂之学，都有研究，与黄宗羲、王夫之并称为明末清初"三大儒"。晚年治经重考证，开清代朴学风气，其批判精神及创新思想影响很广，对社会发展有启蒙意义。

Gu Yanwu (1613—1682 AD), a native of Kunshan, Jiangsu, was a great thinker, philosopher, historian and phonologist. He lived in the Ming and Qing Dynasties.

Gu was born into an eminent family. In his youth, he studied diligently and aspired to serve the country with what he learned. But he could not gain an official position and felt that the traditional civil service examination which required writing eight-legged essays was harmful to Chinese scholars. When the Qing army marched southward and attacked China, he joined the anti-Qing campaign voluntarily and was famous for saying the aphorism "everybody is responsible for the fate of the world". Gu advocated that knowledge should be of practical use to society, and put forward the idea that instead of concentrating all power in the emperor, power should be distributed to a group of officials who would rule together.

Gu was accomplished in many areas. Along with Huang Zongxi and Wang Fuzhi, he was revered as one of the "three most outstanding scholars" of the late Ming and early Qing dynasties. Gu's critical and innovative thinking was considered to have enlightened the Chinese society.

忠清明道救世图

Jie Xuan 揭 暄

少负奇才里巷间，生逢末世作为难。
满怀心血何由洒，百卷兵经一大观。

智不备于一人，谋必参诸群士。
——［明］揭 暄

揭暄（公元1613年—公元1695年），字子宣，号韦纶，别名半斋，明末清初江西广昌人，军事理论家、天文学家、哲学家和数学家。

揭暄出生于读书家庭，少有奇才，品学兼优，喜论兵，慷慨自任。曾与其父衷熙等举义兵，在闽、赣边境抗击清。因向南明唐王（绍宗）建言天时、地势、人事及攻守战御机要等策被采纳，被授以兵部职方司主事。后隐居不仕清，潜心研究，考据著述，内容涉及军事、天文、历史、地理、哲学等诸多领域，多有创见。尤其《揭子兵法》又称"兵经百篇"，是一部重要的军事名著，被誉为"异人异书"。其科学著述还有《璇玑遗述》（又名《写天新语》）和人性论著《性书》等。

Jie Xuan (1613—1695 AD) was a military strategist, astronomer, philosopher and mathematician who lived in the Ming and Qing Dynasties. He was a native of Guangchang, Jiangxi.

Jie was born into a scholar family. As a child, he showed great talents and good character, and was interested in studying military strategies. He and his father once led a troop to fight against Qing forces in Fujian and Jiangxi. Jie offered many suggestions on military affairs to the Prince of Tang of the Ming dynasty and was appointed the chief military official of Ming. In the reign of Qing, Jie would not pursue an official career and focused on academic study. He took interest and contributed in various areas including military, astronomy, history, geography and philosophy. His best-known work is *Jiezi Bingfa* (Art of War by Jiezi).

揭暄著兵法图

Liu Rushi 柳如是

国有危难舍小家，深明大义众人夸。
浮沉世运堪咨嗟，幸得诗书伴生涯。

江城子·忆梦
［明］柳如是

梦中本是伤心路。芙蓉泪，樱桃语。满帘花片，都受人心误。

遮莫今宵风雨话，要他来，来得么。

安排无限销魂事。研红笺，青绫被。留他无计，去便随他去。

算来还有许多时，人近也，愁回处。

柳如是（公元1618年—公元1666年），本名杨爱，字如是，号河东君，以佛典中有"如是我闻"之语而号"我闻居士"，浙江嘉兴人，明末清初名妓，秦淮八艳之一。

其夫钱谦益为东林党首领，南明礼部尚书，后降清，仍为礼部侍郎。虽然身处脂粉之地，柳如是却倜傥自如，不但工于书法，诗词也有较高造诣。因其才貌出众，获得当时陈子龙等著名人物的青睐。公元1632年，柳如是流落松江，改旧名，自号"影怜"，表浊世自怜意。在松江与复社、几社、东林党人交往，常着儒服男装，文与诸人纵谈时势、和诗唱歌。明亡，柳劝钱殉节，钱推托不允，如是奋身投入荷花池，身殉未遂。钱降清后遭忌被逐回乡，钱氏家族乘机逼索柳如是，河东君投缳自尽，年四十六岁。

Liu Rushi (1618—1666 AD) was born in Jiaxing, Zhejiang. She was a renowned courtesan of the late Ming Dynasty and was known as one of the "Eight Beauties of Qinhuai River".

Liu's husband, Qian Qianyi, was initially an official of the Ming Dynasty, but also held important positions in the imperial court of Qing. Liu was noted for calligraphy and poetry and was admired by many eminent scholars. Liu was known for her fondness for dressing in men's clothing and exchanging ideas on social affairs and literature with men. After the collapse of the Ming dynasty, Liu tried to persuade her husband to commit suicide and martyr himself to the fallen Ming, but Qian refused. Liu then attempted suicide by drowning herself in a lotus pond but did not succeed. Later, Liu and Qian were banished to their hometown after Qian was dismissed. After Qian's death, his family attempted to extort money from Liu and she finally hanged herself and died at 46.

如是吟诗图

Zheng Chenggong 郑成功

忠心日月大明身,浴血东南十五春。
驱逐外夷还宝岛,英名长在海之滨。

复 台
[明] 郑成功

开辟荆榛逐荷夷,十年始克复先基。
田横尚有三千客,茹苦间关不忍离。

　　郑成功(公元 1624 年—公元 1662 年),名森,又名福松,表字明俨、大木,为东宁王朝的开国君王。郑成功原为中国南明政权的大将军,因蒙南明绍宗赐明朝国姓朱,赐名成功,世称"国姓爷"。又因蒙南明昭宗封延平王,称"郑延平",尊称"延平郡王"等。

　　1645 年清军攻入江南,不久芝龙降清、田川氏在乱军中自尽;郑成功乃率领父亲旧部在中国东南沿海抗清,成为南明后期主要军事力量之一,一度由海路突袭、包围清江宁府,但终遭清军击退,只能凭借海战优势固守海岛厦门、金门。公元 1661 年正月,郑成功决定出兵收复台湾。荷兰殖民者凭借"坚船利炮"和堡垒进行顽抗,在高山族人民的大力支持下,郑成功击败了荷兰殖民者派来的援兵,经过 8 个月的斗争,收复了"赤嵌城",龟缩在"台湾城"的荷兰总督揆一在 1662 年 1 月 28 日缴械投降,台湾收复。

Zheng Chenggong (1624—1662 AD), also known as Koxinga, King of Tungning, was initially a military general of the Ming Dynasty. He was awarded with the imperial surname "Zhu" and was therefore commonly called the "Lord of the Imperial Surname." His another honorary title was "Prince of Yanping".

Zheng was loyal to the Ming Dynasty and led the fight against the Qing troops on China's southeastern coast. His forces won many battles against Qing but were at last defeated and forced to retreat. Zheng then built a strong defense on the islands of Xiamen and Jinmen. In January 1661, Zheng led his troops to attack the Dutch colonists in Formosa (now Taiwan) and, in alliance with the aboriginal tribes, defeated the Dutch troops. On 1 February 1662, the Dutch Governor of Formosa, Frederick Coyett, surrendered Fort Zeelandia to Zheng.

郑成功收复台湾

Liang Zhangju 梁章钜

一生官宦一生文，博学雄才罕见闻。
独创楹联成别体，清辞朴雅著风云。

题平山堂联

[明] 梁章钜

高视两三州，何论二分月色；
旷观八百载，难忘六一风流。

梁章钜（公元1775年—公元1849年），字闳中，清代福州（祖籍长乐）人，政治家、楹联学家、诗人。

梁章钜出生于书香世家，入仕后曾任礼部员外郎、内廷方略馆编修等，后历湖北、江苏、山东、江苏、甘肃、广西等地方官，每到一地，重视民生，治水赈灾、兴办学校，重视教化，深受百姓拥戴。其与林则徐一同抗英禁烟。

梁章钜一生为官，但在案牍之余却博览群书，勤于著述。能诗善书，学识渊博，精鉴赏，富收藏，好金石，谙掌故，善小品。著作等身，共75种，其中集大成而且有着划时代意义的是楹联学，著有《楹联丛话》等系列专业书籍，收入联话600余则，联作万余，开创了联话体例，确立了分类原则，总结了历代对联成果，保存了珍贵史料。其是国粹楹联学的开山之祖。

Liang Zhangju (1775—1849 AD), a native of Fuzhou, was a politician, scholar and poet of the Qing Dynasty.

Liang was born into a scholar family. In his official career, he served in the imperial court and was later appointed as the local officials of Hubei, Jiangsu, Shandong, Gansu, Guangxi, etc. He endeavored to improve people's livelihood at every place he governed and was adored by the people. He fought together with Lin Zexu in the anti-opium campaign.

Liang read extensively while serving as an official and was a prolific writer. Among his many works, his study of Chinese couplets was of most significance. His works, including *Yinglian Conghua* (Remarks on Selected Couplets), comprised more than 600 commentary articles on couplets and collected more than ten thousand couplets. Liang was considered the founder of Chinese couplet studies.

章钜撰联图

Zhu Da 朱耷

已属神仙道上人，清风不带半分尘。
挥毫落纸无余墨，简洁明了守扑真。

墨点无多泪点多，山河仍旧是山河。
横流乱世权椰树，留得文林细揣摩。

——［明］朱耷

朱耷（公元 1626 年—公元 1705 年），明末清初画家，中国画一代宗师。本名朱统𨨗，字雪个，号八大山人、道朗等，汉族，江西南昌人。

他是明太祖朱元璋第十七子朱权的九世孙，本是皇家世孙。明亡后削发为僧，后改信道教，住南昌青云谱道院。擅书画。花鸟以水墨写意为主，形象夸张奇特，笔墨凝练沉毅，风格雄奇隽永；山水师法董其昌，笔致简洁，有静穆之趣，得疏旷之韵。擅书法，能诗文，用墨极少。朱耷一生坎坷，曾一度精神失常，痛定思痛后，他选择背过身去，与世隔绝，在创作中安放自己孤独的灵魂。

Zhu Da (1626—1705 AD), born in Nanchang, Jiangxi, was a painter of the late Ming dynasty and the early Qing Dynasty. He is known as a great master of Chinese painting.

Zhu was a descendant of the imperial family of Ming. After the Ming Dynasty was overturned, he became a Buddhist monk and later converted to Taoism and lived in a monastery in Nanchang. Zhu excelled in ink wash painting and was famous for his paintings of flowers, birds, and landscape. He was noted for vividly capturing the expressions and postures of birds with a few brushstrokes, and sketching the trees and rocks in swirling, tortuous calligraphic movements. Zhu's life was full of frustrations and he suffered from mental illness for a time. He then focused on painting to distract himself from the misery of life.

八大作画图

Gong Zizhen 龚自珍

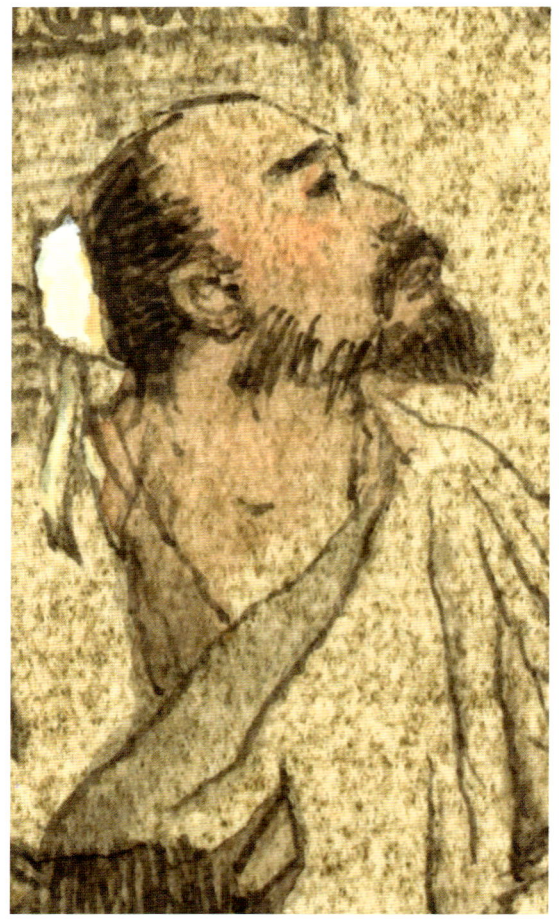

腐朽朝堂岂自珍，辞官归去洁心身。
民生国事安能释，政见诗文一代新。

己亥杂诗（其五）

[明] 龚自珍

浩荡离愁白日斜，
吟鞭东指即天涯。
落红不是无情物，
化作春泥更护花。

龚自珍（公元 1792 年—公元 1841 年），字璱（sè）人，号定庵，清代仁和（今浙江杭州）人，晚年隐居昆山。思想家、诗人。

龚自珍出生于世代官宦之家，少有才名。曾任内阁中书、宗人府主事和礼部主事等职，主张革除弊政，抵制外国侵略，全力支持林则徐禁除鸦片。曾撰写多篇时政论文，指出社会腐败，提出应对之策，未被采纳，辞官南归。其诗文洋溢着强烈的爱国情怀。著有《定庵文集》，存文 300 余篇，诗词近 800 首。著名诗作《己亥杂诗》300 余首，多咏怀和讽喻之作。其中"九州生气恃风雷，万马齐喑究可哀。我劝天公重抖擞，不拘一格降人才。"对沉闷保守的社会状态发出大声呼喊，冀以惊醒人们，为探索民族复兴、国家富强之路而努力。

Gong Zizhen (1792—1841 AD) born in Hangzhou, Zhejiang, was a thinker and poet of the Qing Dynasty.

Gong was born into an official family, and began to display his talents as a kid. He served as the secretary in the Grand Secretariat and the chief official on the Board of Rites and Ceremonies. Gong advocated reform and opposition to foreign aggression, and was a staunch supporter of Lin Zexu and the anti-opium campaign. He wrote many articles to criticize corruption and give advice on social affairs, but his opinions were not adopted by the government. He later resigned and went back to his hometown. Gong composed a total of 300 articles and nearly 800 poems. His works were compiled into *Collected Works of Ding'an*. He was also known for the work *Ji Hai Miscellaneous Poems* which comprises over 300 poems. In his poems, Gong expressed his concern about the society and sought to alert the Chinese in confusion and encouraged them to strive for the prosperity of their country.

自珍归乡图

Pu Songling 蒲松龄

居士生平命运奇，连年八股未相宜。
潜心野史传闻趣，志鬼言妖自立碑。

浣溪沙
[清] 蒲松龄

旧向长堤缆画桡，
秋来秋色倍萧萧，
空垂烟雨拂横桥。
斜倚西风无限恨，
懒将憔悴舞纤腰，
离思别绪一条条。

蒲松龄（公元1640年—公元1715年），字留仙，一字剑臣，别号柳泉居士，世称聊斋先生，自称异史氏，现山东省淄博市淄川区洪山镇蒲家庄人。

蒲松龄出生于一个逐渐败落的中小地主兼商人家庭。19岁应童子试，接连考取县、府、道三个第一，名震一时。补博士弟子员。以后屡试不第，直至71岁时才成贡生。为生活所迫，他除了应同邑人宝应县知县孙蕙之请，为其做幕宾数年之外，主要是在本县西铺村毕际友家做塾师，舌耕笔耘近42年，直至1709年方撤帐归家。公元1715年正月病逝，享年76岁。创作了著名的文言文短篇小说集《聊斋志异》。郭沫若曾这样评价："写鬼写妖高人一等，刺贪刺虐入骨三分。"

Pu Songling (1640—1715 AD), was born in Zibo, Shandong.
Pu was born into a landlord and merchant family. At the age of 19, he ranked first at the local, prefectural, and provincial examinations and became famous in his hometown. But he failed to pass the next level of the imperial exam for decades and it was not until he was 71 that he received the Gongsheng degree. Pu served as a counselor of Sun Hui, magistrate of Baoying County for years, and spent most of his life working as a private tutor. He retired and went back home in 1709 and died of illness in 1715 at the age 76. Pu's most famous work was *Liaozhai zhiyi* (Strange Stories from Liaozhai's Studio), a collection of short stories. He was widely praised for his achievement in literature.

松龄采风图

Cao Xueqin 曹雪芹

巨著红楼纳百科，纤云曲水泛烟波。
脂膏燃尽浮生虑，回首开篇道士歌。

访妙玉乞红梅

[清] 曹雪芹

酒未开樽句未裁，寻春问腊到蓬莱。
不求大士瓶中露，为乞嫦娥槛外梅。
入世冷挑红雪去，离尘香割紫云来。
槎枒谁惜诗肩瘦，衣上犹沾佛院苔。

　　曹雪芹（公元1715年—公元1763年），名沾，字梦阮，号雪芹，又号芹溪、芹圃，祖籍辽宁铁岭，生于江宁（今南京），中国古典名著《红楼梦》作者。

　　曹雪芹出身清代官宦世家，早年在南京江宁织造府亲历了一段锦衣纨绔、富贵风流的生活。曾祖父曹玺任江宁织造，兼任两淮巡盐监察御使，极受康熙宠信。公元1728年，曹家因亏空获罪被抄家，曹雪芹随家人迁回北京老宅。曹雪芹深感世态炎凉，对封建社会有了更清醒、更深刻的认识。他蔑视权贵，远离官场，过着贫困如洗的艰难日子。曹雪芹素性放达，爱好广泛，对金石、诗书、绘画、园林、中医、织补、工艺、饮食等均有所研究。他以坚韧不拔的毅力，历经多年艰辛，终于创作出极具思想性、艺术性的伟大作品—《红楼梦》。曹雪芹是中国历史上最杰出的文学家之一。

Cao Xueqin (1715—1763 AD), also called Cao Zhan, was born in Jiangning (now Nanjing). He was the author of the great classical novel *Dream of the Red Chamber*.

Cao was born into an official family and lived a wealthy life in Jiangning when he was young. His great-grandfather, Cao Xi, was favored by Emperor Kangxi and served as the Commissioner of Imperial Textiles in Jiangning. In 1728, Cao's family was charged with mismanagement of funds and their properties were confiscated. Cao then relocated to Beijing with his family. The incident changed Cao's views on the feudal society. He was refrained from pursuing an official career and lived an impoverished life ever since. Cao had a wide range of interests including poetry, calligraphy, painting, architecture, etc., but was best known for his work *Dream of the Red Chamber*, widely considered China's greatest novel ever. Cao is thus thought to be one of the greatest novelists in Chinese history.

雪芹著书图

Shi Tao 石 涛

山水漫游寻自我，高僧意兴不和同。
奇峰列就心中稿，墨法云云一画通。

题画诗

［清］石涛

冷淡生涯本业儒，家贫休厌食无鱼。
菜根切莫多油煮，留点青灯教子书。

　　石涛（公元 1642 年—公元 1708 年），清初画家，原姓朱，名若极，广西桂林人，祖籍安徽凤阳，小字阿长，别号苦瓜和尚、瞎尊者等，法号有元济、原济等。南明元宗朱亨嘉之子，与弘仁、髡残、朱耷合称"清初四僧"。

　　石涛是中国绘画史上一位十分重要的人物，他既是绘画实践的探索者、革新者，又是艺术理论家。有人称石涛是中国绘画史上屈指可数的伟大人物之一，从他的绘画技艺和理论等方面看确是当之无愧的。他的艺术主张和绘画实践对后世产生了重要影响，也为中国画向近、现代的发展作出了重要贡献。所作凡山水、花鸟、人物、走兽无不精擅且富有新意，尤以山水画及其论著《画语录》名闻天下，把他看成清代以来 300 年间第一人的说法，看来并不过分。

Shi Tao (1642—1708 AD), born in Guilin, Guangxi, was a painter in the early Qing Dynasty. He was a descendant of the Ming imperial family and was known as one of the "four monk painters of the early Qing Dynasty". Shi was one of the most celebrated painters and theorists in Chinese history. He made innovations in the techniques and theories of Chinese painting and his pre-modern landscape style had a strong influence on many Chinese painters. Shi excelled in many genres, including landscape, bird-and-flower painting and figure painting. He was most known for landscape painting and his work *Huayu Lu* (Comments on Paintings). Some considered Shi the greatest Chinese painter ever since the Qing Dynasty.

石涛作画图

Zheng Banqiao 郑板桥

不守陈规不适时，诗书画印见新奇。
官纱脱去衙斋虑，石竹随心着叶枝。

郑板桥（公元 1693 年—公元 1765 年），原名郑燮，字克柔，号理庵，又号板桥，人称板桥先生。江苏兴化人，祖籍苏州。

康熙秀才，雍正十年举人，乾隆元年（1736 年）进士。官山东范县、潍县县令，政绩显著，后客居扬州，以卖画为生，为"扬州八怪"之一。郑板桥一生只画兰、竹、石，自称"四时不谢之兰，百节长青之竹，万古不败之石，千秋不变之人"。其诗书画，世称"三绝"，是清代比较有代表性的文人画家。著有《郑板桥集》。

沁园春·恨
[清] 郑板桥

花亦无知，月亦无聊，酒亦无灵。把夭桃斫断，煞他风景；鹦哥煮熟，佐我杯羹。焚砚烧书，椎琴裂画，毁尽文章抹尽名。荥阳郑，有慕歌家世，乞食风情。

单寒骨相难更，笑席帽青衫太瘦生。看蓬门秋草，年年破巷，疏窗细雨，夜夜孤灯。难道天公，还箝恨口，不许长吁一两声？癫狂甚，取乌丝百幅，细写凄清。

Zheng Banqiao (1693—1765 AD) was a native of Xinghua, Jiangsu. Banqiao was his literary name, but was better known than his birth name Zheng Xie. Zheng passed the imperial examination in 1736 and served as the magistrate of Fan County and Wei County in Shandong Province. He later lived in Yangzhou and sold his paintings to earn a living. Zheng was known as one of the "Eight Eccentrics of Yangzhou" and was noted for his drawing of orchids, bamboo and stones. He was also an influential calligrapher and poet. He authored Collected Works of Zheng Banqiao.

板桥观竹图

Lin Zexu 林则徐

衷情一片几炎凉,不以身心祸福伤。
南海天山同誓愿,终无私欲故成刚。

即 目
[明] 林则徐

万笏尖中路渐成,远看如削近还平。
不知身与诸天接,却讶云从下界生。
飞瀑正拖千嶂雨,斜阳先放一峰晴。
眼前直觉群山小,罗列儿孙未得名。

林则徐(公元1785年—公元1850年),字元抚,又字少穆,晚号俟村老人等,清代福建侯官(今福州市区)人,政治家、思想家、诗人。

林则徐出生于教师家庭,少小懂事有见识。为官后勤勉,历任要职,为国为公。广东禁烟后,反被革职,赴戍伊犁。与妻离别诗"苟利国家生死以,岂因祸福避趋之"以明志。在伊犁服役5年,仍以国事为重,实地勘察,提出"防塞论",指出沙俄威胁终为患。重新启用后任云贵总督,维护了云南边境安定。

林则徐一生力抗西方入侵,但对于西方的文化、科技和贸易则持开放态度,主张学其优而用之,着力翻译西方报刊和书籍,主编《四洲志》,后人称其为放眼世界第一人。林则徐的品格和诗文为后人称颂,如"海纳百川,有容乃大;壁立千仞,无欲则刚"成为人们的座右铭。

Lin Zexu (1785—1850 AD), born in Houguan, Fujian (now Fuzhou, Fujian), was a statesman, thinker, and poet of the Qing Dynasty.

Born into a scholar family, Lin was sensible and perceptive as a child. He served in many important positions and had always been a devoted and just official. He launched the famous anti-opium campaign in Guangdong but was later dismissed and exiled to the remote town Yili. In his poem *For My Family on My Journey to Yili*, he wrote "Were it to benefit my country I would lay down my life; What then is risk to me?" which is his best-known quote. During his five-year exile in Yili, Lin studied national defense and proposed that Russia could pose a threat to China. He was later appointed Viceroy of Yun-Gui and managed to maintain peace at the border.

While he was committed to defending China against foreign aggression throughout his life, Lin advocated opening up and learning from the west. He translated many western newspapers and books into Chinese and compiled *Sizhou Zhi* (Gazetteer of Four Continents). He was called "the first person to see the world with open eyes". Lin's patriotism and literary works have won popular acclaim from Chinese people.

元抚禁烟图

Wei Yuan 魏 源

放眼全球为国强，荣今变古学夷长。
精心海志无人问，可叹当朝闭户场。

花前劝酒吟

[清] 魏源

细雨濛濛江汉宽，楚天无际倚阑干。
水为万古无情绿，酒是千龄不老丹。
故国鱼兼莼菜美，新霜人共菊花寒。
楼船楼阁俱雄壮，黄鹤黄龙醉里看。

魏源（公元1794年—公元1857年），名远达，字默深，又字墨生，号良图，清代湖南邵阳人，思想家、学者。

鸦片战争中毅然投笔从戎，入仕官至知州。魏源主张变法，推崇民主，兴办实业，倡导学习西方先进科学技术，提出"师夷之长技以制夷"的观点。

魏源受林则徐的嘱托，晚年潜心著述，在林则徐主持编译的《四洲志》基础上，经十几年时间完成《海国图志》100卷。此书记述了世界各国的地理、历史、经济、政治、军事和科学技术，乃至宗教、文化等情况，并附有地图。对强国御侮、匡正时弊，振兴国脉作了有益探索，给封闭的国人带来全新的观念。可惜未被当朝重视，而日本获之如至宝，对"明治维新"有巨大影响。

Wei Yuan (1794—1857 AD), born in Shaoyang, Hunan, was a thinker and scholar of the Qing Dynasty.

Wei began his official career during the Opium War and served as the mayor of Gaoyou. He was an advocate of reform and democracy and promoted the development of industry. He also proposed that the Chinese learn the superior technology of the westerners so as to deal with their challenges.

Wei was devoted to writing works in his later years. He spent over ten years on writing his best-known work *Haiguo Tuzhi* ("Illustrated Treatise on Maritime Countries"). Comprising one hundred volumes, the book introduced geography, history, the economy, religion, culture, military affairs and modern science technology of various countries in the world and contained numerous maps. It was an eye-opener for Chinese people and insightful exploration on how to strengthen the nation, but did not receive much attention from the Qing government. The work had a deep impact on Japan and its Meiji Restoration.

魏源著书图

Zeng Guofan 曾国藩

狂澜力挽报清廷，无奈王朝已槁形。
大略宏才难演绎，遗留末代一文星。

> 天下古今之庸人，皆以一惰字致败；
> 天下古今之人才，皆以一傲字致败。
> ——［清］曾国藩

曾国藩（公元1811年—公元1872年），初名子城，字伯涵，号涤生，清代湖南长沙府（今湖南省双峰）人，政治家、军事家、学者。

曾国藩出身于书香门第，自幼勤奋好学。太平天国运动时，曾国藩组建湘军，力挽狂澜，屡立战功，是为晚清重臣，官至两江总督、直隶总督、武英殿大学士，封一等毅勇侯，谥号"文正"。与李鸿章、左宗棠、张之洞并称"晚清中兴四大名臣"。曾国藩多才善谋，洞察时势，倡导"洋务运动"。其创办的安庆军械所，仿造西式枪炮，是中国最早的近代军工业，为近代工业化开了局。曾国藩在政治、军事、学术诸方面均有见解，为后人崇尚。

Zeng Guofan (1811—1872 AD), born in Changsha, Hunan, was a statesman, military general and scholar of the Qing Dynasty.

Zeng was born into a scholar family and had been hardworking since childhood. He was credited with organizing the Xiang Army and suppressing the Taiping Rebellion. He served in important positions including Viceroy of Liangjiang, Viceroy of Zhili, and Grand Secretary of Wuying Hall. He was rewarded with the noble peerage "First Class Marquis Yiyong" and was given the posthumous name Wenzheng. Being one of the four most famous officials of the late Qing Dynasty, Zeng was known for his strategic perception. He established Anqing Armory which produced western-style weapons. It was the earliest modern military factory in China and initiated China's industrialization. Zeng was acclaimed for his perception in politics, military, literary, etc.

曾国藩造像

Li Hongzhang 李鸿章

一品乌纱岂省心，神州内外正消沉。
谁知学士胸中苦，委屈千般何处吟。

舟夜苦雨
[清] 李鸿章

一月天何醉，四山云若痴。
潮添积雨后，春到寒江迟。
梦觉客衾薄，灯昏邻笛悲。
流年孤艇送，不觉鬓丝丝。

　　李鸿章（公元1823年—公元1901年），安徽合肥肥东人，本名章铜，字渐甫，号少荃（泉），晚年自号仪叟，别号省心。晚清名臣，洋务运动的主要领导人之一。

　　李鸿章作为淮军、北洋水师的创始人和统帅，洋务运动的领袖，晚清重臣，建立了中国第一支西式海军北洋水师。因其尽忠辅清，才干了得而闻名。官至东宫三师、文华殿大学士、北洋通商大臣、直隶总督。曾经代表清政府签订了《越南条约》《马关条约》《中法简明条约》等。日本首相伊藤博文视其为"大清帝国中唯一有能耐可和世界列强一争长短之人"。与曾国藩、张之洞、左宗棠并称为"中兴四大名臣"，与俾斯麦、格兰特并称为"十九世纪世界三大伟人"。死后赠太傅，晋一等肃毅侯，谥文忠。著作收于《李文忠公全集》。

Li Hongzhang (1823—1901 AD), born in Hefei, Anhui, was a famous politician and diplomat of the late Qing dynasty. He was one of the leaders of the Self-strengthening Movement.

Li established the Beiyang Fleet, the first western-style navy in Chinese history. He was known for his loyalty to the Qing dynasty and political skills, and served in important positions including Grand Secretary of Wenhua Hall, Beiyang Trade Minister, the Viceroy of Zhili, etc. He signed the Treaty of Shimonoseki and treaties with French on behalf of the Qing government, and was acclaimed by the then Japanese Prime Minister Ito Hirobumi for his diplomatic skills. Along with Zeng Guofan, Zhang Zhidong and Zuo Zongtang, he was one of the four most famous officials of the late Qing dynasty, and was considered to rank with Otto von Bismarck and Ulysses S. Grant. He was posthumously honored as First Class Marquis Suyi and was awarded the posthumous name Wenzhong. His works were collected in *Complete Works of Li Wenzhong*.

鸿章兴邦图

后记 Postscript

朋友张山东，写了一百首咏古诗，让我画些插图放在他的诗集中为其增添少许色彩。我与他是君子之交，义不容辞，便应答下来。

山东较我大八岁，经历也比我丰富得多：我高中毕业后作为知青下放农村务农，他退伍回乡务农，后来都上了大学，都留校当了老师。我教了一辈子书，他后来步入仕途：从事干部理论教育，经济、党务、政务、司法等管理工作，阅历颇丰。

山东在大学学中文专业，毕业教古典文学，虽半生从政，倒也没忘记写诗撰楹，效古代贤达，琴、棋、诗、书都做得出色，尤古体诗，儒风十足。又因其成长于五代南唐画家董源故里，对绘画十分欣赏。他出过几本书，封面都是我设计的。百首诗中的古代人物，其实我也耳熟能详，凭几十年的连环画功夫，画十几幅插图倒也得心应手。但本人生性偏执，凡做事都去较真，总想把想做的事做得没有遗憾，便把原来自家书架上的书翻了个底朝天，又到街上找了一家最大的书店，买了两捆书放到画案上。每画一个人物都去翻阅相关的书籍，查找资料。帮我拎书的学生笑我：这些东西网上有的是。我不领会，只顾在这些书籍里去考究人物的形象、服饰、性格、故事和历史背景，觉

My friend Zhang Shandong is the creator of the one hundred tribute poems in this book. When he asked me if I would draw a few illustrations to add color to the book, I felt duty-bound to do it for my old friend.

Shandong is eight years my senior and has a wider range of experiences than me. We have both worked as a peasant in the countryside: I was sent to the countryside as an "educated youth" after high school while he returned home and worked in the fields after finishing his military service. We have both gone to college, and have both taught at the college after graduation. I remain a college professor today while Shandong has managed to switch to a successful and varied career in politics. He has worked in cadre education, economics, party affairs, administration, justice, etc.

Shandong studied Chinese literature at college. Although he has worked for the government for half his life, he is never rusty in literature and arts. He is an all-round artist and writes extraordinarily good ancient-style poems. Besides, born in the hometown of Dong Yuan, the famous painter of the Southern Tang dynasty, he had great admiration for painting and have invited me to design the covers of some of his books. When I got this offer, I felt I knew the historic figures he wrote about pretty well so drawing their portraits would not be too demanding a task. But being a perfectionist by nature, I rummaged through

得踏实。

完成了山东的任务，觉得不过瘾，总想把事情做到极致，又将诗中的100个人物全部画了一遍。还觉得不过瘾，便邀了几个搞历史的朋友一起，对所有的历史人物进行了一次全面的疏理，再遴选出50个人物，用了近一年的时间，完成了这本文图并茂的画传体图书。

执意去完成这么庞大的绘画创作，也不完全是为了"过把瘾"，而是出于对中国传统文化和历代贤达的敬仰与崇拜。其实这个想法由来已久，只是山东把这"隐"勾了出来。我想无论是谁，只要走进浩如烟海的中国历史长河之中，都会心甘情愿地"淹死"在里面，其博大精深，着实让人忘我，足以使所有有一点血性的华夏子孙为之感慨，为之自豪。我竭尽全力来完成这一艰巨而庞大的创作工程，且生出一种从未有过的责任感和使命感。咏炎黄风骨，颂古国风尚，作为一个有担当的中华儿女，当然更是义不容辞。

纵观五千年中国文明史，书中的150位历史人物，仍然只是沧海一粟。这些英雄豪杰、仁人志士，与中华文明的产生与发展、华夏民族的兴衰与崛起戚戚相关，他们才是我们这个伟大民族的精英和脊梁。无论

my bookshelves for all the references I could find. I then went to the largest bookstore nearby, bought two big piles of books, and put them on my desk so that I was able to research on each of the figure thoroughly before I started to paint them. My students who helped me carry the books to my studio laughed at me and said I could find all the information on the Internet, but I stuck to my printed books. As I read the stories of the figures, I thought about how they should look like, what clothes they should wear, and what personalities they should have. I felt fulfilled doing it.

After completing what Shandong asked for, I got somewhat addicted, as I always am, to my painting assignment, so I carried on and painted portraits of all the one hundred figures that Shandong had composed poems for. Still feeling like doing more, I brought together some historian friends and we spent nearly another year before finishing all the paintings presented in this book.

Deep down I knew that it was really my esteem for my culture and nation that had driven me. I had wanted to do something similar for quite a while. Shandong giving me the mission was just a final push. I believed whoever had had such immersion in Chinese history would have been overwhelmingly impressed and made fiercely proud of the nation as I have. When I worked on this book wholeheartedly, I felt a strong sense of responsibility that I

是政治家、军事家、科学家、文学家，还是哲人、医家、诗人、画家，哪怕一个木匠、一位织娘，只要放在当时的世界历史背景中的任何一个领域去评判，都可堪称巨人。他们为人类的发展与进步所做出的巨大贡献，无以伦比，足以让我们这些后人为之汗颜！书中每一个人物的事迹都是一部英雄史诗，每一个故事与情节都如此惊心动魄，每一个历史瞬间都令人刻骨铭心。我看到一个关于文天祥英勇就义的故事：清人对他行刑，以锯为刑具，刽子手不知如何下手，文天祥居然赐教：板夹之。这是一种何等的气概！一个怎样的旷世豪杰！为国家捐躯，泰然自若，为民族存亡，视死如归。而这种壮举又数不胜数：司马迁为追求史实忍受宫刑，伍子胥为报效天下拒救自刎，周亚夫为忠君护国绝食而终……他们均不是为了个人私利，只求民族大义，家国天下。每每想到这些，我都彻夜难眠。在创作的过程中，我不知多少次把感动与激动的泪水强忍，全身心地投入到绘画创作之中。尽管如此，我仍然不知多少次感到创作的力不从心，用也许难以胜任的绘画技法去表现如此伟大的人物与历史事件而怯怯生畏。即便是当所有的作品完成之后，仍然感到不安、遗憾与不堪承受之重。

had never had before. It is duty-bound for every proud Chinese to glorify the heroes and culture of their nation.

Although the 150 figures depicted in this book are merely a drop in the ocean compared to China's five thousand years of history and civilization, their life has been closely intertwined with the fate of their country. Among them there are politicians, strategists, philosophers, scientists, physicians, scholars, artists, craftsmen, and even textile workers, but all of them, regardless of status, deserve to be called the "backbone of the nation" rightfully because all of them have made massive contributions to the nation. As I read about their lives, I felt that every life is an epic, and every epic is mind-blowing. I read a story about Wen Tianxiang: when he was about to be executed by the Qin dynasty, the executioners did not know how to use the saw and Wen even gave them instructions. What an unequalled hero! He sacrificed his life to his country and faced death bravely. Such glorious deeds abound in Chinese history: Sima Qian endured the humiliation of castration to finfish his great work Records of the Grand Historian; Wu Zixu refused to be rescued and committed suicide out of loyalty to his state; Zhou Yafu went on hunger strike and died for his king and homeland. All of them sacrificed themselves in the interests of their nation. I could not sleep every time I thought about them and I could not remember how many

/ 中国古代150位历史名人画传 /
ZHONGGUO GUDAI 150WEI LISHI MINGREN HUAZHUAN

任何文学艺术的表达与呈现都是有限的，与这些泣鬼神的旷世贤达和惊天地的英雄豪杰相比，都会显得苍白无力。但无论如何，竭尽全力地去做一件自己想要做而且必须去做的极其有意义的事，也算尽了自己一份应尽的责任和义务。但艺术与文学的力量又是巨大的，我相信，一个人用心灵去进行的艺术创作一定可以打动更多人的心灵。至少可以通过这些画作和诗文唤起人们对中国传统文化和民族翘楚的景仰之心。

正值一个新时代的开端，应该又是一个英雄辈出的时代，一个重新唤起国人自尊、自信、自强、自豪的时代，一个民族复兴的时代，但愿这些小小的画作和诗文，在这条澎湃的历史长河中能够溅起一朵小小的浪花，这是我创作这些画作的初衷。

我想这也是山东和为这本书的出版付出辛勤劳动的主编与编辑们的初衷，是所有支持帮助我进行这些作品创作的领导和朋友们的初衷。

2018年8月

times I had been pushed to the verge of tears while painting, and I was constantly overcome by the fear that my paintbrushes are not qualified to portray such honorable characters. The fear, unease and heaviness persisted even after I finished all the painting.

Literature and arts have limitations: our poems and paintings pale in comparison with the glorious deeds of the national heroes. Nevertheless, I found it rewarding to do something that is both my duty and desire. Literature and arts are convincing: I believe the fruits of our strenuous efforts can connect to the readers and ignite their reverence for their country's traditional culture and their most distinguished compatriots.

We are now at the dawn of a new era, an era of national heroes, self-confidence, and rejuvenation. I sincerely hope that this book will give our nation a boost on its journey toward greater prosperity. This has been my intention the whole time.

I think I share this intention with Shandong, Yinan and all the editors who have worked so hard on *Backbone of the Nation*, and all my leaders and friends who have provided support and help.

Wang Xiaoshu

August 2018